Before Being

Before Being

A METAPHYSICAL INQUIRY INTO NOTHINGNESS,
BECOMING, AND THE MYSTERY OF BEING HUMAN

by

Don Howard, MD, PhD

Before Being: A Metaphysical Inquiry into Nothingness, Becoming, and the Mystery of Being Human

Copyright © 2025 by Don Howard

First Edition
Published in the United States of America by
Vibrant Ages Publishing
Mercer Island, Washington

Library of Congress Control Number: 2025917225

ISBNs:
Hardcover (cloth with dust jacket): 979-8-9929178-7-1
Hardcover (case laminate): 979-8-9929178-6-4
Paperback: 979-8-9929178-5-7
eBook: 979-8-9929178-4-0

For more information, visit: www.vibrantages.com or www.vibrantages.org
For inquiries, contact: time@vibrantages.com

Printed in the United States of America

Disclaimer

This book is a work of philosophical reflection and metaphysical inquiry. It is intended to explore questions of existence, meaning, and reality from a personal and intellectual perspective. The content is not offered as scientific, medical, psychological, or theological advice, and should not be interpreted as such. Readers are encouraged to engage critically and thoughtfully with the ideas presented.

Dedication

To Ioulia—
whose life with mine is its own answer to the
question of why anything exists at all.

And to M. V. Nery—
whose gift was not of things, but of the beginning.

Author's Note

I majored in philosophy as an undergraduate at Boston University while also completing my premedical studies. The two paths ran in parallel, often in tension—one practical, structured, and future-facing; the other open-ended, disquieting, and quietly consuming. I didn't always know what to make of that split, but I knew I couldn't give either one up.

It was during those years that metaphysical questions took root—not as academic exercises, but as something intimate and persistent, shaping how I understood time, meaning, and the strange fact of existence. That formative immersion, more than any person or class, stayed with me.

Decades later, I was invited to deliver the commencement address to Boston University's graduating philosophy class. It felt less like a return and more like arriving at the place where something had been waiting all along—a recognition, a reemergence.

The question was not new. But I was finally ready to hear it for what it was: not just why something exists, but whether anything ever could—and if so, whether that something had been given, not simply emerged.

I am grateful for the challenges and complexities that shaped my path. Without them, I might never have learned how to live with the question at the heart of this book.

I didn't expect to write this book. But over time, it became the mystery where the question I had carried for decades finally began to find its form. If it is a kind of magnum opus, it's not because it claims authority, but because it comes from a long and quiet persistence—the most sustained attempt I've made to live with something I still do not fully understand.

When I told my father I'd changed my major from biology to philosophy, he asked, "What are you going to do with a degree in philosophy?"

I said, "Go to medical school."

He laughed.

Epigraph

*"The most sublime question in all of philosophy is:
Why is there something rather than nothing?"*
—GOTTFRIED WILHELM LEIBNIZ

*"What is your substance, whereof are you made,
That millions of strange shadows on you tend?"*
—WILLIAM SHAKESPEARE, *SONNET 53*

Table of Contents

Preface

The question came quietly. Not as a hypothesis, but as a disturbance. It surfaced over time—and remained.

At fifteen, I was drawn to philosophy by a restless desire to understand: consciousness, morality, time, the origin of things. I believed, as many do, that the deepest questions would yield answers if pursued far enough.

As a doctoral student in science and medicine, I began to see something else: that in science, we do not ask, "What is the answer?" We seek the right question, trusting it will shape the experiment—and the experiment, the answer. The question begets the answer.

Years later, I spoke to a group of philosophy graduates at my alma mater. In that address, I posed five questions I had come to believe were worth carrying. But afterward, I realized I had missed one—the one that had been with me all along, just beneath the others. Perhaps the deepest. It hadn't arrived that day; it had been waiting. Not as a conclusion, but as a lingering disturbance. And it stayed.

The idea that became this book began to take clearer form about a decade ago, during a voyage to the Galápagos Islands. Surrounded by signs of Darwin's vision—raw nature, adaptation, contingency—I found myself thinking not only about life, but about existence itself. I had brought with me two books: Jim Holt's *Why Does the World Exist?* and Sean Carroll's *The Big Picture*. Both were thoughtful, and each offered insight into how the universe might be understood—scientifically, cosmologically, even philosophically. But something still felt unresolved. The question that pressed on me was not just why there is something rather than nothing—but what, exactly, do we mean by "nothing"? What kind of nothing could truly precede being—and could anything emerge from it? It was not the answers in those books that stayed with me. It was what they left open.

The question beneath the question stayed with me. Not as a project, but as a pressure—a sense that something essential had not yet been fully asked, and that nearly every system of thought either avoided it, reframed it, or assumed it had been answered. I carried that sense privately until it began to take shape on the page.

This is not a personal book. But it is, in some sense, a personal act. It comes from a long interior apprenticeship to something that does not let go. It is not a work of theology or science. It does not offer answers. It is an effort to stay with the mystery long enough to see what it reveals—not by being solved, but by being followed.

The question begins on the far side of certainty. It does not ask to be answered—but it asks to be lived with.

Prologue

There is a question that comes before all others. It does not follow from evidence. It is not prompted by experience. It does not arise from curiosity about how the world works, or how life began, or how minds evolved. It comes before world, before life, before mind.

Why is there something rather than nothing?

It is not a puzzle to be solved. It is not a gap in scientific understanding or a placeholder for what we don't yet know. It is the absence of anything that could be known. The question stands on the threshold where thought reaches the end of what it can compare.

Most of the time, we live after the question has already been deferred. The world appears, and we assume it. We study its patterns, we name its forces, we live and lose and grieve within its shape. But underneath all of it—beneath time, beneath law, beneath presence—is the fact that anything exists at all.

This book begins there.

Not with a hypothesis, but with the refusal to look away. With the sense that this question is not only legitimate, but inescapable. That it is not unanswered, but foundational. That it may never yield to reason, but it may still demand a response.

There is no way to begin without stepping into strangeness. But the strangeness is not foreign. It is intimate. It is what every structure presupposes, and what no explanation can eliminate. It is the one question that cannot be asked from within the world it questions.

It is posed at the boundary of that world—not a location, but a limit where our faculties, our capacities, fall silent.

What follows begins with a definition of nothing, stricter than any conventional scientific, theological, or philosophical use. It is not emptiness or absence, but the utter negation of all structure, all potential, and all ground for being. No entities. No laws or logic. No time or place. No possibility. No necessity. This—together with the inquiry it sets in motion—is a point of departure distant from those traditions. It will serve as the ground from which everything to come unfolds.

PART I
The Question

How Do We Begin from Nothing?

CHAPTER 1

No Where, No When, No How

The Meaning of Absolute Nothingness

We use the word "nothing" often—sometimes flippantly, sometimes with a quiet gravity.

There's nothing more to be said.

I feel... nothing.

It all came from nothing.

But what do we really mean?

Usually, "nothing" is a stand-in for absence. An empty room. A silent night. A vacuum with no particles, no matter. But even these contain structure. The room has space. The silence passes in time. The vacuum obeys laws. These are not nothing. They are something—pared down, stripped back, but still nested within the frameworks of being.

Even in the realm of science, what's often called "nothing" turns out to be a stage full of subtle activity. A quantum vacuum—the lowest-energy state of a field, still alive with fluctuations—may be devoid of matter, but it still hums with possibility. Virtual particles flicker into and out of existence. Fields oscillate. Mathematics operates. Rules apply.

So if we want to ask the question—Why is there something rather than nothing?—we have to be much more careful with our terms. We have to be willing to let go of nearly every assumption that language, logic, and habit hand us. Because the kind of "nothing" we're talking about here... is radical.

It's not empty space. It's not silence. It's not even stillness. Those things all exist within some context: they occur in time, occupy dimensions, follow rules. What we mean instead is the absolute absence of anything and everything—not just of stuff, but of structure. No matter. No energy. No dimensions. No distance. No time in which anything could unfold. No laws to constrain or allow. No logic to give coherence. No modal facts—facts about what could or must be—no possibility, necessity, or probability. No mathematical landscape shaping potential outcomes. No potential at all.

No where. No when.

No how.

Not even a void. That word suggests a container. This is the absence of container and content alike. A condition—not even that—a non-condition so complete it leaves no room for contrast. No shadow. No silence. Not even the idea of absence.

Try to picture it—and you'll fail. We all do. Our minds reach reflexively for images: a blank screen, a black expanse, a kind of mental fog. But these are still something. They still imply space, depth, a viewer.

The truth is: you can't imagine this kind of nothing.

And that impossibility isn't a failure of imagination.

It's a clue.

We are creatures of being. Our thoughts are built on structures—time, relation, form, distinction. Even negation only makes sense inside a system. So when we say "nothing," we keep smuggling in bits of something. We can't help ourselves. The stage keeps sneaking back in.

But the question we're asking requires us to try anyway. It demands that we press past intuition, past imagery, past even coherence. Because to ask *Why is there something rather than nothing?*—and to really mean it—we have to start from the most barren place imaginable.

We have to start where imagination breaks.

This is not the "nothing" of physics, which often conceals something—a quantum vacuum, a fluctuation, a set of boundary conditions. It is not the "nothing" of analytic philosophy, which approaches it from within an inherited logical framework. Nor is it the fertile emptiness of certain religious or philosophical traditions—for example, the Kyoto School's "absolute nothingness," which denotes a generative or spiritually inflected ground of meaning. The nothingness meant in this inquiry is absolute: it has no place, no power, no latent capacity. It is the absence of any absence.

Reduced to its strictest terms, it is this.

Absolute nothingness, as defined here, is a *boundary-concept*—not a state, and not the "boundary conditions" of a system, as in physics, but the outermost edge of thought, where no system, framework, or rule apply. It is the utter absence of entities, properties, laws, logic, modal facts, potentials, time, and place. It marks a limit beyond which explanatory grammar has no reach. Words like "holding," "enduring," "failing," or "collapsing" are used only to guide thought toward that limit; they do not ascribe qualities or powers to nothingness.

The claim is that such nothingness could not obtain—not by rule or by probability, for at this threshold no rules apply—but because there is no basis for absence to sustain itself as absence. Absolute nothingness, in its strictest sense, offers no ground for persistence; there is nothing in it to preserve its own non-being. At that limit, the question changes: if it could not hold, in what manner could being arise?

From that vantage, only two possibilities remain, and they are unavoidable. Either being arises from within that absence, as an inherent instability that cannot suppress itself, or it comes from beyond it, as the act or presence of something not bound by that absence at all. Any imagined alternative is only a variation of one or the other: to posit a prior reality is to place it beyond nothingness, and to imagine a fluctuation or emergence within is to place it inside.

Their details will unfold later, yet both arise from the same uncompromising definition, the refusal to soften or reify it, and the conclusion that what could not obtain could not endure—a convergence of definition, consequence, and vision that may never before have been gathered in quite this way.

The Question Behind Every Question

And here's the strange thing: even though we can't picture it, we can still mean it. We can point to it—not with images, but with intention. That impossible absence becomes the background against which all being appears. It's the silence deeper than silence. The void beneath every form. The question before all other questions.

So this is where we begin. Not with theories. Not with physics. Not with gods or creation myths or the history of the universe.

We begin with a kind of nothing so complete that it has no origin, no structure, no resistance—and ask:

Could that have ever truly held?

And if not—why not?

If such a nothing—absolute, unstructured, unconditioned—could ever have existed, we must ask: *Why didn't it stay that way?*

Why should there be something—anything at all—instead of the total absence of everything?

There is no law within true nothingness that can be broken, no principle to violate, no pressure to change. So why change? Why shift from the absence of being to the explosion of it?

And if it did change—if being appeared where before there was not even potential—what does that say about the nature of reality? What does it say about what kind of world we live in, and what kind of beings we are?

These questions aren't abstract riddles. They are razor-edged. They cut through physics and theology alike. They reach beneath every model of the universe, beneath every cosmology and creation myth. Because all of those models begin with some version of "something." A singularity. A quantum field. A timeless entity. A first cause. A divine will.

But this question begins before any of that.

It begins where nothing—not even a beginning—exists.

And that is what makes it so disorienting.

Because it doesn't ask us to understand the universe.

It asks us to understand the absence of all universes.

And here's the irony: we don't really know how to do that. Every tool we have—reason, imagination, mathematics, metaphor—is designed for being. They all presuppose difference, relation, structure. The moment we say, "There was nothing," we've already said too much. We've already framed it, already carved it into the shape of thought.

But even if we can't grasp it, we can stand next to the question. We can let its silence work on us. We can feel, however dimly, the strangeness of the fact that something exists. That we exist. That this page, this moment, this thought—any of it—is happening at all.

Philosopher Martin Heidegger famously called this "the fundamental question." He meant it ontologically—why there is being rather than nothing—as a way of revealing our relation to existence. But the question we're asking here is even starker. Not just why there is being, but why there is anything at all, given that nothing—*true* nothing—could have held. Others have treated this as a curiosity, an intellectual parlor trick. But I disagree. I think it's a real question—perhaps the most real question there is. Because if nothingness truly had no internal necessity, no structure, no force—then being stands exposed. Not as inevitable, not as planned, but as a miracle. Or a failure. Or both.

That's the pivot point.

If absolute nothingness was possible, why didn't it hold?

If it was impossible, why?

What kind of universe are we in, that being exists at all—and keeps existing?

The rest of this book explores two broad answers to that question.

One possibility is that nothingness was unstable—not in the physical sense, because physics doesn't exist yet—but in a deeper way. That its very lack of constraint meant there was nothing to prevent being from erupting. That existence emerged not because it was pushed or chosen, but because there was nothing to stop it.

The other possibility is intention—that being was chosen rather than forced—conceived either impersonally, as intention without a subject, or, on a theistic reading, as intention with a subject: someone who willed there to be being. In many traditions that "someone" is called God, though not necessarily bound to that image and perhaps unlike anything theology or history has imagined. On this view, what exists came into existence because it was wanted. Not accidentally. Not mechanically. But freely. Being is not merely a fact—it is an act.

We'll explore both views. We'll press into their implications. And we'll return, again and again, to the question that animates them.

Why is there something rather than nothing? And—if something must exist—why this? Why order, beauty, love, consciousness, decay, longing, memory, death? Why us?

The question doesn't want an answer. It wants a witness.

But before we go further, we need to know how others have asked the question—and how they've failed to ask it fully.

That's where we turn next.

What "Nothing" Is Not

First, we need to sweep away the debris.

Because nearly every time someone has tried to answer this question—Why is there something rather than nothing?—they've done so by redefining what "nothing" means. Sometimes the shift is subtle. Sometimes it's flagrant. But either way, the result is the same: the question gets answered, but only by cheating.

Let's start with science.

In many popular accounts of cosmology, we're told that the universe arose from "nothing"—as if that were a tidy solution. But if you read closely, the nothing they describe is already loaded. It includes quantum fields, energy fluctuations, mathematical symmetries. In some versions, it's a vacuum governed by the laws of quantum mechanics. In others, it's a timeless equation from which space and time emerge. But in every case, there's something there: a backdrop, a potential, a structure. Rules. Relations. Possibility.

It's not nothing. It's a pregnant silence—a silence already humming with the potential for music.

This is not a criticism of physics. Physics is designed to describe what can be measured, modeled, and predicted. It is not in the business of describing the absence of law or the negation of possibility. And that's fine—as long as we're clear about it. When a physicist says "nothing," they often mean a very low-energy state within a structured system. Fair enough—it's simply a different question.

But if we're going to ask the metaphysical question—why anything exists at all—we can't borrow the language of science and pretend it answers it. You can't explain existence by appealing to laws that only make sense once existence already is.

Theology, too, has its own sleight of hand.

In many traditions, the universe is said to have been created *ex nihilo*—"from nothing." But again, if you look closely, you find a presence lurking: a creator, a will, a mind—something prior. The "nothing" is not really nothing. It may be the absence of material, but it is not the absence of purpose. The divine remains, fully formed, ready to act. There is no true void—only a waiting.

This may be a rich and meaningful view, but it is not what we are talking about here. We are not imagining a cosmic craftsman standing outside time, waiting to flip the switch. That is simply more being—located before other being. It shifts the question one step back but leaves the mystery intact.

Even in philosophy, the definition often softens.

Sometimes "nothing" is treated as a logical abstraction—a negation of being. Sometimes it is a placeholder for what we cannot know. Sometimes it is a rhetorical device, an intellectual dark matter used to frame a more familiar idea. In some traditions, it becomes mystical—a space of emptiness suffused with meaning. In others, it is existential—a sense of futility, a gap in the self.

All of these can be powerful in their own way, but they are not the thing we are after. They do not take the question far enough. They still leave room for law, for potential, for experience. They still smuggle in some version of something.

What we are seeking is more radical—an absence that does not contain even the capacity for being. Not the emptiness out of which things might emerge, but the condition in which emergence itself has no meaning. No spacetime. No background field. No dimensionality. No clock. No sequence. No "before." No observer. No framework in which anything might stir, or fall silent.

Not a place that is empty.

Not a force that is dormant.

Not a silence waiting to break.

But the total absence of any place, any force, any silence, any break.

And once we have removed all that—once we have pushed past physics and myth and metaphor—we arrive at something we cannot see, but which we can still ask about.

What if this condition—this radical nothing—really could have existed?

And if so... why didn't it last?

The Impossibility of Imagining Nothing

Let us admit something at the outset: we cannot fully picture what we are talking about.

We can define true nothingness. We can describe what it is not. We can use language to outline the edges of absence. But we cannot imagine it—not purely, not without smuggling something in.

Every attempt conjures traces of being: some sense of space, some dim volume, some vantage point. We might picture a black expanse, an infinite fog, a blank screen with the brightness turned all the way down. But these are metaphors with the furniture stripped away. They still imply space, contrast, orientation. They still rest on the scaffolding of being.

Even the idea of *absence* assumes a reference point: something that once was, or could be, or should be. The moment we say "nothing," we have already imported the grammar of something. We cannot help it. We are creatures of relation, shaped by structure, encoded by time. Our minds are formed by difference and boundary. Even erasure only makes sense against a backdrop that allows something to be erased.

Push further. Try to imagine not a black void, but the absence of void. Not silence, but the absence of the very conditions that make silence possible. Not emptiness, but no space in which emptiness could reside. No rules to suspend. No background to strip away. No logic to violate. No dimension in which anything might begin—or fail to begin.

You cannot do it. Neither can I. And this is not a personal limitation; it is a cognitive fact. No part of the human brain evolved to simulate non-being. Every tool we possess for thinking—every metaphor we devise, every abstraction we construct, every image we summon—assumes contrast. It assumes form. It assumes presence, even if only in negative space.

And yet this failure may itself be instructive. It tells us something—not yet about the world, but about ourselves. We are not neutral observers. We are participants in a reality that has already begun. We are made of being. We live inside time. We communicate through difference. So when we attempt to imagine nothingness—true nothingness—we are trying to simulate a condition from which we ourselves are excluded. A condition with no "we," no space to occupy, no mind to imagine, no process to unfold.

In that sense, the attempt is doomed from the start, because imagining is already something.

And yet we try. Why?

Because even if we cannot visualize it, we can gesture toward it. We can recognize what it would have to be, even if we cannot hold it in thought. We can subtract and subtract until nothing is left to take away. And when we reach that vanishing point, we can still ask:

Why did it not remain that way?

If true nothingness is not only unimaginable but unstable—if it gives way, spontaneously, to being—then something remarkable has occurred. Something metaphysical. Something foundational.

It would mean that being is more real than non-being. That reality, once impossible to suppress, emerged not because it was forced, or chosen, or caused—but because there was simply nothing to prevent it.

That is one possibility.

The other is equally strange: that being exists because it was intended. That something—or someone—willed there to be being, and made it so. Not as a decision within time, but as a timeless act. A gift. A freedom. A will.

We will come to both of these soon. But before we follow those paths, we must first understand how this question has been asked before—and why those earlier attempts have all fallen short.

Why Precision Matters

There is a temptation, even among thoughtful people, to wave the question away. To say, "Of course something exists—we are here, aren't we?" Or to sidestep: "Maybe the universe just is. Maybe the question itself makes no sense."

But such replies often rest on a lack of precision. Or worse, they proceed as if the key term—*nothing*—were allowed to drift, undefined, ambiguous, clothed in borrowed meanings.

That is why we have labored to sharpen it.

Because if *nothing* simply means empty space, or the absence of matter, or a pre-physical vacuum governed by mathematical law, then the question of why something exists becomes a matter of technical explanation. And technical explanations begin *after* something already is.

We can describe how fluctuations might give rise to particles, how time might emerge from entropy gradients, how complexity might form in the wake of symmetry-breaking. But none of these accounts answers the deeper question. They only relocate it.

Any explanation that begins with structure—any structure at all—has already begun with something. And every something, no matter how elegant, invites the same question:

Why is there that, rather than nothing?

CHAPTER 2

The Question That History Refused to Ask

How the Absence of Being Was Deferred, Reframed, or Denied

I f we were to ask the ancient philosophers what they thought of "noth-ing," we would likely have been met with a puzzled look—if not outright dismissal. Among them, the Eleatics—Parmenides and his followers—were the most uncompromising: for them, non-being was not only suspect—it was considered unintelligible.

Parmenides, writing in the 5th century BCE, rejected the very notion that nothing could exist. His logic was spare and uncompromising: What is, is. What is not, is not. And from that, he drew a bold conclusion: the idea of nothingness is incoherent. There is no becoming, no change, no empti-ness. Being is eternal, undivided, unshakable. It simply is.

It was more than a curious doctrine; it struck at the heart of every-day experience. For Parmenides, even motion was illusion—dramatized by Zeno's paradoxes: the arrow, motionless at each instant and thus never truly in flight; and Achilles, who must always cover half the remaining dis-tance to the tortoise and so, in theory, never overtakes it. Birth and decay, movement and transformation were not reality, but deception. Only un-changing being could be thought; all else—what we see, touch, and experi-ence—was mere opinion, never truth.

And he meant it. For all its starkness, Parmenides' view wasn't a thought experiment. It was a metaphysical certainty grounded in logic: You cannot speak or think about what is not. Therefore, it cannot be. The possibility of nothing—true nothing—was ruled out from the start.

This was no eccentric outlier; it became a cornerstone of early metaphysics. Plato, in his dialogues, imagined reality as layered and hierarchical—a world of eternal Forms casting the shadows we see. Yet even at his most abstract, radical nothingness never enters the scene. In the *Sophist*, "not-being" is recast as difference, not sheer nonexistence; in the *Timaeus*, the *chōra*—the pre-cosmic "receptacle"—is a formless, pre-ordered medium, not an absolute absence. For Plato, the lack of form is disorder, but it is never the complete negation of being.

Aristotle approached the question with a more empirical and systematic mind. He allowed for potentiality, for things to emerge or pass away, but always from something—matter, motion, or form awaiting determination. He rejected the physical void and treated "non-being" chiefly as privation (*sterēsis*), a lack within being rather than its total negation. His "prime mover," the unmoved source of all motion, was eternal. In both Plato's and Aristotle's systems, nothingness in the radical sense was not absent—it was inconceivable.

A rare change in tone—but not in substance—came with early atomism. In the 5th century BCE, Democritus envisioned a universe built from indivisible particles—atoms—drifting through a background void. This void was no true nothingness, but an empty space that made motion possible. Even in this early nod toward absence, nothingness was treated as functional rather than foundational, framed within an existing structure rather than the collapse of one.

The Pythagoreans, with their more mystical bent, saw reality as grounded in number and proportion. Some even spoke of a "void" entering the world to separate things—not absolute nothing, but a structural ingredient woven into the cosmos. To them, the universe was never chaotic but quietly ordered, a hidden harmony beneath appearances. In both the Pythagorean vision and the atomists' world, there is no encounter with total absence—always something, whether atoms or ratios, moving, shaping, and operating behind the scenes.

For these thinkers, to speak of "nothing" was either a category error or a poetic flourish. The world might shift and change. Things might perish. But being, as a whole, never truly goes away.

This isn't just a technical position. It reflects a deep metaphysical instinct—one that remained largely unchallenged for centuries. The idea that something could come from absolute nothingness wasn't unorthodox. It was unthinkable. What existed, existed. And what didn't, didn't. There was no middle ground, and no outside.

In this light, our modern question—Why is there something rather than nothing?—would have made little sense. The priority of being was assumed, not argued. The notion of a "true nothing," as we've defined it, was not part of the conceptual toolkit. And so the absence we're daring to imagine—without time, law, structure, or potential—never even came to the table.

It's worth noting that even outside the West, early traditions approached nothingness obliquely, if at all. In early Daoist thought, the Dao was described as the source of all things, a generative silence from which form emerges—but it was not conceived as absence. In classical Indian philosophy, "voidness" sometimes appeared as a negation of attributes, but not as ontological nonexistence. And in early Buddhism, speculation about cosmic origins was often set aside as unhelpful. Emptiness (śūnyatā) was central, and emphatically not nihilism—it meant the absence of inherent nature (svabhāva) through dependent origination, not the absence of existence.

These approaches, for all their insight, still leave us short of the cliff's edge. They reach toward mystery, but do not define the absence of all being. They offer negation, but not the absolute collapse of all potential, all presence, all rule.

If the ancient world had a concept of "nothing," it was provisional. Always tethered to being. Always shadowed by something more stable.

The radical nothingness we're exploring—a silence without any space for sound, a void without the frame of a void—was not yet on the philosophical map.

But it would come. Slowly, and with hesitation.

The refusal to entertain true nothingness left a kind of conceptual scar. Western metaphysics would spend millennia circling around being—measuring it, classifying it, refining it—but rarely daring to ask whether it might have been otherwise. The question didn't evolve. It waited.

The Theological Turn: Creation, but Never Emptiness

If early philosophy circled around being, theology placed it in the hands of God. The central question became not whether there is something rather than nothing, but who willed it into being.

In the Judeo-Christian tradition, the doctrine of creation ex nihilo—creation "out of nothing"—emerged gradually, becoming explicit in late Second Temple Judaism and early Christian sources. It affirmed divine sovereignty: God did not shape a pre-existing chaos but brought being into existence through will alone. In this view, the universe is contingent—dependent on something beyond itself.

But as daring as this sounds, it still leaves "nothing" strangely full.

In theological cosmology, the absence of material does not imply the absence of agency. God remains—a presence before all presences, a will prior to all structure. In this framework, "nothing" is not the absence of everything; it is simply the absence of created things. Purpose, power, and possibility are still there. The divine mind waits, timeless and active, ready to speak the world into being.

So even when "nothing" appears in sacred texts or theological creeds, it is not true nothingness. It is more like a pause between intentions, a silence that is part of a larger score. It presumes a hidden composer.

This tension continues in the writings of Augustine, who emphasized that time began with creation, and that nothing preceded it—not even time. He was, in that sense, ahead of many modern cosmologists. But he

never imagined a state without God. In Aquinas, being is rooted in necessity, with God as *ipsum esse subsistens*—being itself. Contingent beings require a cause, but that cause is always anchored in an uncaused cause. God
is not in time, but not absent. God is not a thing, but not nothing.

Some later thinkers within the Christian tradition pushed further toward the edges of metaphysical speculation. Duns Scotus introduced the
idea of a "formal distinction" within God's attributes—seeking to explain
how infinite being could manifest in diverse forms. Nicholas of Cusa spoke
of the "coincidence of opposites," where the maximum and the minimum
meet, where unity holds multiplicity without contradiction. These were
profound steps into the outermost reach of conceptual thought. But even
here, nothingness was not entertained as a real condition. Being was infinite, mysterious, self-folding—but never absent. The divine remained, if
not definable, then irreducibly there.

In Islamic philosophy, we find a similarly layered view. Thinkers like
al-Fārābī, Avicenna, and later al-Ghazālī spoke of the Necessary Existent—
an eternal, self-sufficient source from which all contingent beings flow.
Avicenna's proof of the Necessary Existent placed God not just as creator,
but as the metaphysical foundation of existence. This, too, is a vision in
which being is grounded in something outside the cosmos, but not outside
structure. There is always logic, always hierarchy, always a reason.

In Jewish mysticism, especially within the Kabbalistic tradition, there
is the notion of *Ein Sof*—the Infinite, which precedes creation. The *tzimt-
zum*, or divine withdrawal, makes room for creation by concealing part of
the Infinite. Within Kabbalistic thought, whether this withdrawal is literal
or metaphorical remains debated, but either way it is not a true absence. It
is a veiled fullness. The divine never vanishes; it only retreats.

Even in Eastern traditions, where metaphysical frameworks differ,
true nothingness is rare. In Vedantic philosophy, the cosmos unfolds from
Brahman, an undivided, infinite consciousness. In early Buddhism, the concept of *śūnyatā*—emptiness—is central and is emphatically not nihilism; it
refers to the absence of inherent nature (*svabhāva*) in phenomena, grounded

in dependent origination, not to non-being. In Daoism, the Dao is the generative ground of all things, a fertile silence—but never a literal nothing. The Dao cannot be named, but it is not absent. It is the source.

What all these traditions have in common is this: they never let go of the idea that something must exist. The word "nothing" may be invoked, but it is quickly surrounded—by spirit, by reason, by necessity, by will. There is no moment, no gap, no ontological zero.

This is not a flaw. These are rich and complex systems of thought, grappling with questions of creation, contingency, and purpose. But they are not asking what we are asking.

We are not starting with God as the world understands God. We are not asking whether divine intention can explain the cosmos. We are asking something prior to that: Could there have been absolutely nothing? Not even God? Not even the capacity for God?

In that sense, the theological traditions—while profound in their own right—stop short of the void. They imagine a universe made by a mind, but never a state in which mind itself was impossible—where not even logic could prevail, and where being had no source because being, in any form or possibility, did not exist at all.

That's the difference.

And it matters. Because if even theology cannot conceive of a reality without structure, then we must ask: Is this because such a reality is unthinkable—or because we have never truly dared to think it?

Early Modern Philosophy: Necessary Being and the Retreat from Absence

In the early modern period, the question of existence began to shift. With the decline of medieval scholasticism and the rise of rationalist and empirical philosophy, metaphysical inquiry became more rigorous—but also more constrained. The question "Why is there something rather than nothing?" surfaced explicitly in this era, but even then, it never reached the depth we are attempting here.

Gottfried Wilhelm Leibniz is often credited with posing the question in its most famous form: "Why is there something rather than nothing?" For Leibniz, this was no idle curiosity. It was the most foundational question of all. Yet his answer came quickly and was tightly bound: there must be something because something must exist necessarily. And that something, he argued, is God—a perfect, non-contingent being whose existence explains the existence of everything else.

Leibniz framed his reasoning through the Principle of Sufficient Reason—the idea that for anything that exists, there must be an explanation for why it is so and not otherwise. "Nothingness," he admitted, would have been simpler than this world. But because this world exists, there must be a sufficient reason for its existence. For Leibniz, that reason could not lie within the world itself; it had to lie beyond it. And so he posited a God who not only explains the fact of being, but chooses the best of all possible worlds (*Principles of Nature and Grace*).

It's a clever solution. It preserves rational order. It protects the elegance of metaphysical logic. But it also closes the door almost immediately. "Nothing" exists in the thought experiment only long enough to be dismissed. It is never taken seriously as a real possibility. It is introduced, in effect, only to be defeated.

Baruch Spinoza, a contemporary of Leibniz, offered an even starker view. For Spinoza, God and Nature are one and the same—an infinite, necessary substance from which all else follows. There is no room for contingency, no metaphysical silence, no primal decision. Everything that exists does so because it must—not because it was chosen or permitted, but because it flows necessarily from the nature of being itself.

In Spinoza's universe, non-being is not just rejected—it is irrelevant. There is no conceivable alternative. The cosmos is simply the self-expression of substance. It does not begin. It does not risk. It does not not-be.

The contrast between Leibniz and Spinoza is instructive. One preserves the possibility of a divine chooser; the other removes the chooser altogether. But both ultimately banish nothingness. Whether through rational selection or metaphysical necessity, being is assumed to be more fundamental than its absence. The question—Why is there anything at all?—gets either redirected or swallowed up in system.

René Descartes, often seen as the father of modern philosophy, approached the question from a different angle. His goal was not to explain the origin of being, but to secure the foundation of knowledge. His famous *cogito*—I think, therefore I am—was intended to establish certainty beneath doubt. But even this rests on the presence of being. The thinker exists. The doubt exists. The deceiver—real or imagined—exists. The void never arrives.

Later figures like David Hume and Immanuel Kant further shifted the focus. Hume distrusted metaphysical speculation altogether, treating cause and effect as habits of thought, not guarantees of reality. Kant, meanwhile, acknowledged the limitations of human reason in grasping the ultimate origins of things. We can know the world as it appears, he argued, but not as it is in itself. These insights are profound—but they stop short of the abyss. The idea of true nothingness, unconditioned by perception or law, was not their concern.

These thinkers were wrestling with foundational problems: contingency, necessity, causation, knowledge, the limits of reason. Their contributions were real, lasting, and in many cases brilliant. But they did not ask what we are asking.

Where there might have been a confrontation with the sheer absence of being, they substituted principle. Where there might have been silence, they offered logic. Where they might have stepped into the void, they fortified their systems.

And so, once again, the question retreated. *Why is there something rather than nothing?* became a doorway that was shut just as it began to open. Being was declared necessary, whether by divine perfection, infinite substance, or the inevitability of consciousness.

But what if it isn't?

What if being isn't logically inevitable? What if no necessity explains the fact that anything exists at all? What if the most basic truth is not that something must be—but that it might just as easily have never been?

That possibility wasn't seriously entertained in the early modern period. In a sense, it couldn't be. The intellectual climate was still too tethered to theological scaffolding, to rationalist confidence, to metaphysical formalisms.

There was no space yet for the terrifying honesty of the void.

But that space would begin to open in the centuries ahead. And when it did, the question would return—not as a logical problem to be solved, but as a presence. An undertone. A silent wound.

Existentialism and Phenomenology: Nothingness as Mood, Gap, or Gesture

Martin Heidegger, one of the most influential philosophers of the 20th century, famously referred to "the nothing" not as an absence of everything, but as an ontological backdrop—a presence that reveals being by contrast. In his 1929 lecture *What Is Metaphysics?*, he writes that the nothing "nihilates"—it makes the presence of beings appear by withdrawing. This "nothing" is not true non-being. It is not the absence of logic, time, space, or possibility. It is more like a clearing, an opening through which being discloses itself.

It's an evocative idea. But it is still tethered to being. Heidegger's nothing is not a state. It is an experience—a mood, even. He claims that certain moments, like profound anxiety, bring us face to face with this nothing. But what we encounter isn't void. It's estrangement. A dislocation that arises only because we are already present. (Rudolf Carnap's famous critique of Heidegger targeted precisely this move—treating "nothing" as if it were an entity.)

Jean-Paul Sartre, building on Heidegger, treated nothingness as something internal to consciousness. In *Being and Nothingness*, he writes that human awareness is defined not by what it contains, but by what it lacks. To be conscious is to be aware of not being something else. This nothing is productive—it allows us to negate, to choose, to become. Sartre's "nothingness" is the gap between what we are and what we could be.

But again, this is not the absence of being itself. It is the space within being for freedom and failure. It is existential distance, not metaphysical nonexistence.

Other voices in this tradition, like Maurice Merleau-Ponty and Simone de Beauvoir, continued to explore the fractures within being, but not its absence. Merleau-Ponty emphasized ambiguity and embodiment—how perception is never pure, how meaning is always partial, situated, and unfolding. De Beauvoir extended these insights into the ethical and existential sphere, asking what it means to act and choose within a world that refuses certainty. Their work is profound in its confrontation with ambiguity, freedom, and finitude. But still, the question of being's origin—the possibility that nothingness might have been total, not just experiential—remains untouched. What they explore is fragmentation within existence, not its metaphysical alternative.

We see similar motifs in Albert Camus, who famously described life as absurd—not because it is meaningless, but because it confronts us with the silence of the universe. This silence is emotional, existential. It's not a void in the metaphysical sense. It's a refusal to respond. Camus does not argue that nothingness is real. He argues that meaning is not guaranteed.

In a different register, Paul Tillich, the Protestant theologian and philosopher, wrote about "the threat of non-being" as the root of anxiety. For Tillich, non-being haunts us—not as a thing we encounter, but as a condition we fear. But even he stops short of imagining a world in which being never arrived. His non-being is psychological, spiritual. It makes us tremble, but it never overtakes us.

All of these thinkers approached the edge—but they stopped just short of falling in.

They spoke of negation, absence, estrangement, silence, finitude, anxiety, loss. But they did not speak of a state in which nothing—truly nothing—could have been. They did not press the question into the space where even law and logic fall away.

Instead, nothingness became a texture. A wound inside being. A shadow cast by light.

This shift matters. It gave philosophy new tools for grappling with meaning, identity, and mortality. It reintroduced uncertainty into the experience of existence. But it still didn't ask our question—not all the way.

Because even in anxiety, there is still being. Even in despair, there is a subject to despair. Even in silence, there is the structure of sound held back.

The existentialists gave us a deeper vocabulary for what it means to be fractured, alienated, incomplete. But they left untouched the possibility that nothingness—not psychological or emotional, but metaphysical and total—could have been all there was.

That possibility remains.

And it waits just beyond the last place philosophy was willing to go.

Contemporary Physics and Cosmology: Equations in the Void

In our own time, the question of origins has migrated from metaphysics to cosmology. We are no longer told that God created the world, or that being is eternal and necessary. We are told that the universe emerged from a quantum vacuum, or from a fluctuation in a timeless field, or from a spontaneous symmetry break governed by as-yet-unified laws. "Nothing," we are told, has become something.

But once again, we must ask—what kind of nothing are we talking about?

Modern physics has made extraordinary progress in explaining how the universe evolves once it begins. The Big Bang model, inflation theory, quantum field dynamics, and multiverse hypotheses have all stretched our understanding of spacetime to its limits. But when these theories speak of "nothing," they often mean something that is mathematically empty but ontologically rich.

For instance, when physicist Lawrence Krauss titled his book *A Universe from Nothing*, he described a state that lacks matter and energy, but not the laws of quantum mechanics. His "nothing" includes a vacuum structure, governed by fluctuations in underlying fields. These fields exist, even if what we normally think of as "stuff" does not. They are something—low-activity, rule-bound, silently simmering, but something nonetheless. Philosopher David Albert has sharply critiqued this usage, noting that it retains physical structure under the label "nothing."

In similar fashion, Stephen Hawking and James Hartle proposed a "no-boundary" condition in quantum cosmology, in which time itself behaves like a spatial dimension at the earliest moments of the universe. This eliminates a hard "beginning," but does not eliminate structure. Their version of nothing still requires a mathematical framework that defines how time, energy, and curvature behave.

Even Sean Carroll, who acknowledges the mystery of why the universe exists at all, often frames "nothing" as a high-symmetry state of a quantum wavefunction. It is the simplest state allowed by the rules—but those rules are still there. The wavefunction must be governed by something. The question remains: Why is there that rule, that symmetry, that allowable state?

The problem isn't dishonesty. These are not semantic tricks. These are serious scientists using the best tools available to describe the conditions under which a universe like ours might arise. But those tools are not equipped to describe the absence of all tools.

Physics can describe the conditions under which "something" becomes more something. It can even speculate about how complex structure arises from minimal inputs. But it cannot describe the absence of structure. It cannot explain why the laws exist. It cannot model the condition in which even mathematics fails.

And so, once more, "nothing" becomes a placeholder. It is invoked, defined narrowly, and then replaced by a system—a field, a probability function, a symmetry principle, a geometrical constraint.

But if we ask *Why is there something rather than nothing?*—and if by "nothing" we mean not a vacuum, not a field, not a possible configuration, but the complete absence of being, structure, law, potential, or relation—then none of these explanations apply. They begin too late, starting with assumptions that already smuggle in the very thing we are trying to understand: being itself.

This doesn't mean science is failing. It simply means it is asking a different question.

Science explains the *how* of the universe—how it behaves, how it evolves, how it might have begun. But it cannot reach the *why* behind being itself. It cannot tell us whether being was inevitable, chosen, or simply impossible to suppress.

That is not a failure of science. It is a boundary.

And it is at that boundary that this book begins.

Closing Reflection: At the Threshold

Across centuries of thought—philosophical, theological, existential, scientific—the question has been asked, avoided, redefined, and repackaged. *Why is there something rather than nothing?* has hovered at the edges of language and logic, always threatening to collapse into silence or certainty. Most have not dared to ask it on its own terms. Fewer still have treated "nothing" with the full severity it demands.

The traditions we've explored offer profound insights, but each one begins too late. Each assumes something—an eternal law, a divine will, a necessary substance, a quantum field. Each carries structure hidden in its foundation. None confront the abyss directly.

But what if we did?

This is not a rejection of those traditions. It is a recognition that every one of them—philosophical, theological, existential, scientific—still began with something. With a frame, a field, a logic, a law. The question we are asking now is different. It does not begin with wonder at the world, but with the possibility that no world might ever have been; not wonder at what is, but the refusal to assume it had to be. What if we began not with something, but with nothing—not as emptiness, not as negation, not as silence waiting to break, but as the total absence of law, logic, potential, and place?

What if such a nothing could have existed?

And if so... why didn't it last?

That is the question we turn to next—not as a continuation of the past, but as a metaphysical proposal. And with it, we arrive at the conceptual center of this book: the radical idea that absolute nothingness could not hold.

It is time now to step beyond tradition—and ask what happens when nothing cannot hold.

PART II
The Instability of Nothing

When Absence Fails to Endure

CHAPTER 3

The Inconceivability of Absolute Nothing

Being Without Cause, Constraint, or Design

We've come a long way just to arrive at the place we began. The question—Why is there something rather than nothing?—has echoed through history, reshaped by theologians, softened by philosophers, and repackaged by physicists. But only now are we ready to confront it on its own terms.

This chapter marks a turning point. It offers the core hypothesis at the heart of this book: that absolute nothingness, once clearly defined, could not hold.

To do that, we must return to where we started: to true nothingness—not as emptiness, not as vacuum, not as silence within space, but as the absolute absence of everything. No space, no time, no logic, no law. No potential, no being, no "before," no frame. Not even the conditions for contrast. Not even the idea of absence.

Absolute nothingness, in the sense used here, is a boundary-concept—a conceptual limit—rather than a state, the complete absence of entities, properties, laws, logic, modal facts (facts about what could or must be), potentials, time, and place. It marks the farthest horizon of thought, beyond which explanatory grammar has no reach. Words such as "holding," "enduring," "failing," or "collapsing" are used only to lead thought toward that horizon, chosen with a precision meant to bar even the faintest suggestion of structure, potential, or hidden capacity.

Similarly, phrases such as "from nothing," "nothing stood in the way," or "no law prevented emergence" are scaffolding for readers used to rule-based explanation. They depict neither a pre-system condition nor any permissive power in nothingness, but the complete inapplicability of prevention, permission, causation, and probability at the origin.

This definition stands apart from every treatment that has come before—whether from physics' vacua, the different possible "empty" states in physical theory; from analytic claims that "nothing is impossible" based on modal inference, reasoning about what is possible or necessary; or from traditions that see in nothingness a hidden generative power. It is strict and apophatic—defined only by what it refuses to grant—and, taken with the conclusion that such nothingness cannot hold, yields a concept that has not been assembled in precisely this way before. If it is indeed unique, it is offered not as a last word, but as a vantage from which the most profound question may be seen, and asked, anew.

It is almost impossible to hold in thought—and that is part of its power.

We are not speaking of what came before the universe. That's a temporal idea, and time doesn't apply here. We are not asking what caused being to appear. That assumes a system with cause and effect. We are asking something simpler, and stranger:

Could absolute nothingness have existed? And if so... why didn't it remain what it was?

That's the hinge.

Because if nothingness truly means the absence of all structure, then it cannot include a rule that says "stay as you are." It cannot resist change, because resistance is a function of order. It cannot hold itself in place, because place does not exist.

Could such nothingness have existed? If so, it could not have lasted—not even for an instant—because it lacked the means to preserve itself. But perhaps the truth is starker still: perhaps it could never have been actual at all. The definition remains the same in either case: absolute nothingness is the complete absence of space, time, law, logic, potential, or any means of preservation. Whether reality ever instantiated such a condition is a separate question from what the concept itself entails. If the condition cannot hold, it may also be incapable of arising in the first place, making being not the result of collapse but the default state of reality.

Whether nothingness was fleeting or forever impossible, the outcome is the same: absolute absence is nowhere to be found, and being is here. In either case, existence does not depend on cause, design, or permission. It appears because nothing prevented it—because there was no law, no structure, no constraint to keep it from appearing.

And so we arrive at a possibility that is both terrifying and strangely clean: nothingness is unstable not because of anything it contains, but because it contains nothing at all—not even the capacity to remain unchanged. At this limit, the very notions of capacity and persistence collapse; they have no standing here.

This chapter explores that idea. Not as metaphor. Not as poetry. But as a genuine metaphysical hypothesis. Not that being was caused. Not that it was chosen. But that it emerged—because there was nothing to prevent it, in a context where neither prevention nor permission apply.

Why Absolute Nothingness Cannot Endure

Because with nothing to hold it, absence yields to being.

To say that nothingness is unstable sounds, at first, like a contradiction. Instability implies tension, disequilibrium, potential. It suggests a condition waiting to change.

But this is not what we mean.

We are not proposing that nothingness is like a stretched membrane, trembling until it snaps. That kind of instability belongs to systems—to structures with internal constraints or competing forces. True nothingness has none of that. It has no structure, no tension, no energy, no field. It has no framework within which instability could even occur.

And that is precisely the point.

If nothingness includes no laws, then it also includes no law that says it must remain as it is. No principle of stasis. No prohibition on emergence. No governing logic that demands continuation. It cannot be stable in any defined sense, because there is nothing within it to preserve its state.

Stability, like identity, requires order. It requires something to hold something else in place. But if there is no something, and no "else," then there is also no mechanism—no constraint—that could stop the appearance of being. Not because anything is pushing for it. Not because something breaks through. But because there is no rule left to follow.

This is not instability in the physical sense. In physics, an unstable state is one that tends to evolve into a lower-energy configuration. But physics already assumes a space of possibilities—a system with rules, however minimal. A field of values that can shift. We are speaking here of a situation that precedes all such structures.

And so we must frame the idea differently.

What if nothingness cannot endure not because it's fragile, but because it's unprotected? What if its very lack of order is not a flaw to be overcome, but a condition that cannot hold—not even for an instant—because it offers no resistance to being?

We tend to think of instability as something dynamic—as a condition on the verge of change, held in tension by opposing forces. But that kind of instability presumes structure. It presumes contrast, relation, containment. What we're describing here is something different. In true nothingness, there is no tension, no struggle, no force waiting to act. There is simply no mechanism at all—no rule to prevent change, but also no rule to enforce stillness. In that absence, stasis cannot be sustained. Not because something intrudes, but because nothing protects it. The condition itself fails to secure its own nonexistence. It has no anchor.

There is no contradiction here, only strangeness. Being would not arise from nothingness, as though propelled by a cause. It would arise because there is no cause—and no resistance.

In this view, the appearance of being is not an event. It is not a happening in time. It is not a change within a field. It is a kind of ontological release, not into a space, but into the absence of prevention.

A collapse of non-being into the only thing that remains when nothingness cannot persist: something.

Not Cause, Not Plan, Not Accident

If being arose from true nothingness, we are tempted to explain it. That temptation is ancient. We want to ask: What caused it? What set it off? What allowed it to happen?

But those are the wrong kinds of questions.

Cause implies a system—a rule that connects one thing to another. It presumes time, relation, consequence. Plan implies a will, a chooser, a before and after. Even randomness implies a backdrop against which outcomes can be measured—a field of possibilities, a statistical range, a structure.

But in true nothingness, none of that exists.

There is no time to unfold. No chooser to act. No space of possibilities to randomize.

There is not even a field in which fluctuation might occur. No law of probability. No principle of symmetry to break. No logic to generate alternatives.

So if being emerges, it does not do so by cause, by plan, or by chance. It emerges not because of something, but because there is nothing—nothing to block it, nothing to sustain non-being, nothing to say "no."

It is not an answer. It is not an action. It is what happens when there is no mechanism left to prevent anything at all.

This is not an intuitive idea. Our minds are trained to search for agents, for forces behind every transition. We expect beginnings to have reasons. But this hypothesis denies all of that. It imagines a reality in which the beginning was not permitted, not selected, not rolled like dice—

but simply unresisted.

That is its strangeness. And its simplicity.

Being appears, not because it was meant to, or because it won the odds, or because it was needed. It appears because nothingness has no defense. No law to keep it pure. No constraint to keep it from collapsing into something other than itself.

It is not an act. It is not an outcome. It is not even an error.

It is what remains when non-being fails to remain.

The Ontological Shock of Spontaneous Being

If being appeared not through plan, not through force, not even through chance—but because nothing forbade it—what does that mean for reality?

It means that existence is not the result of a decision, nor the product of necessity. It is not inevitable in the usual sense, because inevitability implies structure. But it is also not accidental in the ordinary sense, because accident requires a backdrop of probability.

It happens, because nothingness—true, radical nothingness—has no means of defending itself. It has no scaffolding. No symmetry to preserve. No state to return to. It cannot enforce its own non-being, because it lacks the logic or law to do so.

This is not the kind of emergence we are used to imagining. It does not involve process, transition, or becoming in time. There is no before and after. There is only a shift—from nothing, to something—not driven by anything, but permitted by the complete absence of resistance.

This is where the shock begins to register.

We are so accustomed to thinking of being as ordered, as intentional, or at least as explained. We expect reasons. We expect coherence. Even absurdity, when we speak of it, is framed against the expectation of meaning. But this—this is not absurd. It is not chaotic. It is not ironic.

It is bare.

To imagine being not as created or chosen, but as the thing that happens when nothingness cannot hold—this is to see existence as neither gift nor accident, but as release. A letting go that is not a decision, but the default when no decision is possible.

And we are what comes after that.

What does it mean to live in a reality that was never secured—never guaranteed, never selected? It means we are not the outcome of a plan, nor the inhabitants of a designed world. We are inheritors of a condition that did not require us, did not foresee us, and does not explain itself to us. That doesn't render existence meaningless. But it does remove the scaffolding of expectation. It means that everything we are—every question, every grief, every joy—emerges in a space that did not ask for them. And that is precisely what gives them weight. Not because they were given, but because they are here, uninvited and undeniable.

We are the echo of being's first unopposed appearance. We are what reality looks like when something has replaced nothing, not because it was meant to, but because there was no law left to stop it.

That realization is more than strange. It is arresting.

Because if this is right, then the universe is not justified. It is not optimized. It is not designed. It simply is.

And so are we.

Resistance to the Hypothesis

This idea—that being emerges because nothing cannot endure—sounds, to many, like sleight of hand. It offends our instinct for order. Surely, we think, something must have *caused* existence. Surely it can't have just appeared.

The most common objection is a simple one:

How can something come from nothing?

But that question carries its own assumptions—assumptions that don't apply here.

It assumes that "nothing" is a kind of background.

It assumes that something was added to it.

It assumes time, sequence, causality, and contrast.

But true nothingness contains none of that. It has no place to add to. No framework to break. No temporal sequence to mark "before" and "after." There is no thing to *become*, and no condition in which becoming makes sense.

So the question *"How can something come from nothing?"* misses the mark. It imagines nothing as an empty container, into which being arrives. But we are not speaking of a container. We are speaking of the absence of containers, the absence of *everything*, including the structure that would make cause and effect possible.

In that absence, the question changes.

We don't ask how something *came* from nothing.

We ask why nothingness didn't remain what it was.

That may still feel unsatisfying. It should. We are trained to think in terms of action and explanation. We expect a trigger, a before, a mechanism. But this hypothesis offers none of that. Its power lies in what it removes. It asks us to imagine the simplest possible condition—absolute absence—and then recognize that such a condition lacks even the stability to preserve itself.

No rule forbids being.

No logic keeps absence pure.

No constraint is there to prevent emergence.

So being happens—not by plan or mistake, but by the failure of nothingness to continue being nothing.

That is not an answer in the traditional sense.

It is a reorientation.

And it requires us to abandon the very kinds of explanation we have always leaned on.

What This Explains—and What It Doesn't

If being emerged because nothingness could not persist, then we've explained something important—maybe the most important thing: that existence does not require a cause. Not a plan, not a will, not even a possibility—just the absence of anything that could prevent it.

That, in itself, is a radical claim. It answers the oldest question with an answer so stark, so stripped down, that we almost want to look away from it. It doesn't comfort. It doesn't narrate. It just... states.

But we need to be clear. This hypothesis—powerful as it is—doesn't explain everything. In fact, it explains very little beyond the bare fact that something exists.

It tells us why being might have happened. But it doesn't tell us why this being happened.

It doesn't explain why the universe has order. Or why its laws are elegant enough to be written in mathematics. It doesn't explain why particles behave in structured ways, or why complexity emerges, or why there is time, or space, or anything like coherence.

It doesn't explain why the universe is intelligible at all.

It also doesn't explain why consciousness appears. Why there are minds. Why there is memory. Why there is longing. Why anything in the universe seems capable of reflecting on its own existence.

And it certainly doesn't tell us why we feel that some things matter. Or why love exists. Or beauty. Or grief.

All of that—the shape and texture of being—is still untouched. This hypothesis offers no blueprint for meaning, no hint of design, no promise of purpose. It gives us only one thing: a way to understand why there is something rather than nothing, without invoking a cause, a mind, or a mistake.

It does not settle the question of meaning. It does not reveal a pattern or declare a purpose. What it offers instead is a narrowing—a conceptual stripping away of everything we thought we needed to explain existence. That stripping away is not reductionist. It is preparatory. Because once the need for origin stories and justifications is removed, we are left with something more exposed, and perhaps more honest: the raw presence of being itself, asking nothing, explaining nothing, and still somehow inviting a response.

That's not everything.

But it's not nothing, either.

It clears the ground. It gives us the barest armature: the possibility that existence is what happens when nothing cannot hold. And from that, we can ask: *If being emerges on its own, with no guidance—what kind of world might follow?*

That is the question we'll begin to explore next.

A Stark Kind of Beauty

There's something unsettling about this view. It offers no comfort, no reassurance, no hidden order. Being, in this hypothesis, wasn't summoned. It wasn't selected. It wasn't meant. It just appeared—because nothingness could not endure.

And yet, for all its austerity, there's a kind of beauty here.

Not the beauty of intention or story. Not the elegance of design. But something colder, quieter, more elemental. A kind of metaphysical honesty.

In this vision, the universe is not a message. It is not a symbol. It is not a gift. It is a release. A collapse. A silent unraveling of absence into something—simply because nothing could keep it from happening.

There is no agency behind it. No narrative arc. No voice calling light into being. And still, here we are—breathing, remembering, asking questions into a space that didn't have to exist.

Maybe that's enough. Maybe the fact that` something is here—not by force, not by need, but simply because it was unopposed—is reason to pay attention. To wonder. To live as though being, even without explanation, is worth inhabiting.

This is not a conclusion. It's not even a position. It's a way of seeing.

A way of standing still before the one thing no system has ever explained:

That something is.

And it could have been otherwise.

If being emerged because nothingness gave way, then everything that has ever existed—every atom, every galaxy, every thought—is the consequence of that first unopposed arrival.

But emergence alone doesn't explain the form being takes.

It doesn't explain why being unfolds in structured ways. Why it doesn't just collapse into noise. Why there are patterns, particles, symmetry, repetition. Why the universe is not just something, but something ordered enough to endure—and, eventually, to wonder.

If nothingness gave way to being by default, then we are left with a second mystery:

Can mathematics emerge from metaphysical silence?

Can logic appear where coherence was never required?

Could order arise from spontaneity—without a mind, without a plan, without a cause?

Did anything shape what followed?

Could what the world understands as God have arisen even after being itself?

That's where we go next.

In the chapters that follow, we'll explore whether the forms we see in the world—its intelligibility, its elegance, its improbable stability—can be explained without invoking design or necessity.

Can the universe build itself?

Here the mystery deepens.

If we are to follow it honestly, we must be precise about what we mean. From this point forward, unless otherwise stated, "nothing" will bear the sense defined in Chapter 1 and developed in Chapter 3—the absolute absence of all structure, law, potential, or ground for being.

Not emptiness, not void, but the lack of any framework in which emptiness or void could even make sense: no time or place, no contrast or relation, no possibility, no necessity, no witness, no modality at all.

CHAPTER 4

When Form Follows Being

How Structure Could Arise Without Origin, Order, or Intent

I f being emerged because absolute nothingness could not persist, we are left with a second mystery. Not just that something exists, but that it exists in such a structured way. The universe did not arrive as chaos. It arrived as something that could be described. It came with pattern, regularity, and stability. The form of being we inhabit doesn't just appear—it holds together.

There are laws, or at least consistencies. Particles behave predictably. Energy transforms in governed ways. Forces interact within knowable boundaries. Even time, as ambiguous as it may be, unfolds with a rhythm. From the level of quantum fields to the rotation of galaxies, reality seems to organize itself around form. It doesn't flail or collapse. It coheres.

And that raises a deeper question: Why is being ordered at all? Why is there coherence rather than formlessness? If absolute nothingness gave way to something not through will, cause, or plan, then structure—the kind we now see everywhere—was not chosen. It wasn't imposed. It wasn't guided. It just arrived.

So why is the universe mathematical? Why is it intelligible?

We take it for granted that physical reality can be described with equations. That logic works. That symmetry exists. But from the standpoint of absolute nothingness, none of this was required. Structure wasn't necessary. It wasn't coded into the absence. There was no scaffolding, no buried seed of geometry. And yet here we are: in a world with dimension, distinction, interaction, and coherence. A world in which shape appears to be integral to the very texture of being.

That's what's strange.

We're not asking why this specific particle behaves as it does, or why a given constant holds its value. We're asking something more primitive: why is there any structure at all, if being emerged from the absence of all form?

If absolute nothingness truly held no principle, no potential, no logic—then what explains the fact that being, once it appeared, did not immediately collapse into noise or dissolve into disorder? Why doesn't it flicker like static, or erupt and vanish without duration? Why doesn't it fracture? Scatter? Fail?

Instead, it endures. It composes. It builds.

Something in being has cohered. And that coherence—the hidden fact of order—is not obvious. It is what we begin to ask about now.

We rarely pause to consider how strange this is. We assume that once being appears, it will persist, take shape, behave. But why should it? Why wouldn't existence, once released from nothingness, erupt into static—brief, violent, and gone? Why wouldn't it flicker across contrastless dimensions, incapable of gathering itself into pattern? A single instant of being might have come and gone, leaving no trace. Or it might have unfolded as pure incoherence: patterns that never repeat, states that never stabilize, no logic, no law, no persistence. Instead, something endured. The first act of being did not fracture or burn out. It held. And that is not an obvious outcome—it is a metaphysical surprise. We are so used to the order we find ourselves in that we forget to ask what made coherence possible in the first place.

The Problem with Eternal Forms

The idea that mathematical or logical forms exist independently of matter has deep roots. In Plato's metaphysics, the physical world is a shadow cast by a more perfect, immaterial realm—a realm of Forms, where the truths of geometry, number, and essence reside. These Forms are not invented or constructed. They are discovered. They exist necessarily, eternally, and without change.

It's a powerful idea. And it's tempting to import it into modern cosmology. If the universe seems mathematical, why not assume that mathematics preceded it? If logic is everywhere, why not believe it was always there?

But that assumption carries a cost.

To place eternal structure outside or before being is to introduce a metaphysical leakage into the void. It implies that the absence we started with—the absolute nothingness that contains no law, no form, no contrast—isn't really empty. That it contains something after all. Not matter or energy, but a hidden framework. A background logic that doesn't count as "something," but still makes structure inevitable once being begins.

That's a contradiction.

Because the moment we allow anything—however abstract, however immaterial—to exist "before" being, we are no longer speaking of nothing. We're speaking of a system. A pre-geometry. A silent code lying in wait. And that means the original absence was not absolute. It was seeded. Structured. Pregnant with possibility.

But absolute nothingness, by definition, permits none of that. No embedded structure. No potential to be revealed. No informational residue, no symmetry, no logic—because logic, too, is a type of order.

This is the problem with eternal forms. As beautiful as they are, they don't stay outside the universe. They sneak in. They imply a mode of necessary being—not as a personal deity, but as an abstract structure that was always there. And once you admit that, you've already left the hypothesis behind.

In this view, being is no longer emergent. It's following a pattern. A design. A law that predates its appearance. But that's not the question we're asking.

We are not trying to explain the world by appealing to what it might have been modeled on. We are trying to understand how it could have emerged when there was nothing to model it, nothing to contain it, and nothing to shape it.

If absolute nothingness is real—if it was not just empty, but void of even the potential for form—then eternal mathematics cannot be part of it. Logic, symmetry, coherence—these must have come later.

And that means structure itself may be part of the eruption. Not a prelude, but a consequence. Something that appears with being, not before it.

Could Form Arise After Being?

If form did not precede being, then it must have followed it. That reversal is not just conceptual—it's metaphysical. It suggests that order, coherence, and logic are not the scaffolding on which reality was built, but something that emerged with being. Maybe not immediately. Maybe not fully formed. But present enough to grow.

It's not an easy idea to absorb. We are used to thinking of form as foundational. As that which gives shape to the world. But in this view, form is not the ground—it is a consequence. It is not that logic governs being, but that once being exists, logic begins to take shape. Once anything exists at all, it can relate, contrast, change. And those contrasts—those differences—are the seeds of pattern.

Being is never pure, because the moment it appears, it introduces distinction. This, not that. Here, not there. With difference comes relation. With relation, the possibility of pattern. With pattern, the birth of order.

In this light, mathematics is not a silent code lying in wait. It is an awareness—an articulation of the relationships that emerge when being divides itself. Geometry arises not because space was always there, but because distance appears as soon as two points can be distinguished. Logic arises not because it is eternal, but because the moment there is contrast, inference becomes possible.

This does not mean that form is random. It means that form is co-emergent—that it grows with being, as being begins to unfold. The patterns we see in the world may feel ancient, but they may be no older than existence.

And maybe not even that old.

Because it's possible that order didn't emerge all at once. That the earliest configurations of being were unstable, disjointed, undirected. That the regularities we now depend on—the laws of physics, the rhythms of time, the elegance of mathematics—settled into place only after being began to stabilize.

In this way, structure becomes not an origin, but a consequence. Not a principle to be obeyed, but a configuration that congeals when being holds long enough to allow order to take root.

That would mean the universe wasn't born with a map. It found its shape slowly, perhaps blindly, as the fact of being unfolded into space, relation, and intelligibility.

Because if logic, mathematics, and structure could emerge only after being began, then the same question could be asked of mind at its most exalted. Could what the world understands as God have arisen after being—emerging not as the cause of reality, but as one of its later possibilities? Or could God have been the very first emergence from nothingness, with all else unfolding from that initial presence? This is only one possibility among others; elsewhere in this chapter, we consider the alternative that what first emerged was a material chaos, which for reasons unknown began to settle into the ordered reality we now inhabit. But if God were the first to appear, the further question would arise: why would God, rather than anything else, be the first to emerge when nothing could not endure? The emergentist view leaves this question open—whether such a mind, if it appeared first, would be a necessity of being itself, or simply one possible way reality could have begun.

Self-Stabilizing Reality

If form did not preexist being, but emerged alongside it—or just after it—then we are faced with a new possibility: that reality has the capacity to settle into pattern. Not by design, and not by external imposition, but through self-organization, inherent in the act of existing.

This idea isn't entirely foreign. We see analogs of it in nature. Crystals form spontaneously in cooling liquid. Snowflakes grow according to rules no one wrote. Simple systems, when left alone, often fall into pattern—not because they are meant to, but because some configurations are simply more stable than others.

Physicists call this symmetry breaking—the idea that a system, even one in a perfectly balanced state, may spontaneously choose a direction, a shape, a structure. Once that break occurs, everything downstream is shaped by it. A field tilts slightly, and that tilt becomes the rule. A vacuum fluctuates, and that fluctuation becomes a universe.

But these are just metaphors. They belong to physics. And physics, as we've seen, already assumes a framework—a set of laws that govern energy, mass, entropy, interaction. The question here is deeper: Could order emerge in the first moment of being—not from law, but from the way being responds to itself?

In the absence of guidance, could reality fall into pattern simply because pattern is what endures?

Once being appears, it does not stay inert. It generates relation. That relation can amplify or cancel. It can echo or collide. Some configurations scatter. Others persist. If being persists long enough to echo itself, it may begin to reinforce its own regularities. Not because it is aiming at stability, but because stability, once it appears, is hard to undo.

This would mean that form does not need to be planted at the root. It can grow outward. It can find itself. Like a landscape settling after eruption, the raw presence of being may begin to quiet itself—not through intention, but through self-compatibility.

And if that's the case, then the ordered universe we inhabit is not the product of a fixed design. It is a consequence of what being becomes when it is left alone—and does not collapse.

Gödel and the Limits of Logic

If structure emerges with being, and if logic arises only when contrast and relation appear, then we must ask a deeper question: How far can logic take us? And more provocatively, does logic explain being—or does it stop just short of doing so?

The modern history of logic changed forever in the early twentieth century, when a young Austrian mathematician named Kurt Gödel published a proof that shattered the dream of a complete and consistent formal system. His incompleteness theorems showed, in essence, that in any logical framework complex enough to include basic arithmetic, there will always be true statements that cannot be proven within the system itself.

This was more than a mathematical result. It was a philosophical rupture. It meant that even the most carefully constructed orders of thought contain blind spots. That truth and proof do not fully overlap. That certainty has edges.

To grasp this more concretely, imagine a vast book that contains every truth about arithmetic. Now suppose you try to write a complete set of logical rules capable of proving all those truths. Gödel showed this cannot be done. No matter how thorough your system, there will always be some truths in the book that your rules cannot reach. And if you try to expand the rules to capture those, new unreachable truths will appear. The system is forever incomplete.

Or think of it another way: as if you're navigating a sealed room with a perfect map of its interior. You assume the map can show everything there is to know. But some features of the room—true features—cannot be revealed from within, no matter how flawless the map. To see them, you'd have to step outside. Yet even then, the new map will carry its own blind spots. The limitation isn't a failure of thought—it's part of what it means to work within any system.

Gödel didn't just show that some truths lie beyond proof. He revealed that every system complex enough to describe arithmetic will generate statements it cannot resolve. And this isn't due to lack of ingenuity—it's baked into the very framework. Any formal system rich enough to be meaningful will, by necessity, be incomplete.

That has consequences far beyond mathematics. It suggests that order comes with internal limits. That every logic we construct—or inherit—will contain truths it cannot reach. And if that's the case, then even our deepest systems of understanding may be bounded by the shape of the reality that generated them. We cannot assume that logic is universal. It may be local. Emergent. A tool that arises with being and stabilizes just far enough to model the structures that endure—but not far enough to explain them fully.

For our purposes, Gödel's result adds something important to this unfolding idea: that even logic may have emerged with limitations baked in. That the rules we now treat as stable, elegant, and universal may not be complete. They may be provisional. Not arbitrary, but contingent—bound not by necessity, but by the specific shape reality settled into when being first appeared.

This doesn't mean logic is flawed. It means it may be local. Emergent. A language formed not to precede being, but to describe its structure after the fact.

It also means that if we are looking for a final explanation for form, logic may not be able to give it. Even as it helps us model form, it may not explain why form exists in the first place. The deeper we dig, the more we begin to suspect that structure may describe reality without fully containing it.

We see something similar in physics. Just as Gödel revealed that certain truths cannot be derived from within a formal system, Heisenberg showed that certain properties of a quantum system—like position and momentum—cannot be simultaneously known. This isn't a matter of practical limitation, but a feature of the framework itself. In both cases, the act of knowing encounters a boundary, not because we are missing information, but because the system does not permit full transparency from within. Whether in logic or physics, something resists total description.

And that brings us to a paradox: the universe may be deeply intelligible, but that intelligibility may not be complete. We may live in a reality that makes sense only up to a point, beyond which coherence gives way to silence.

If that's true, then logic, like mathematics, may not have existed in absolute nothingness. It may have come into being only as being found shape. And even then, it may only go so far.

The Tension Between Order and Openness

The universe is ordered—but not perfectly. It is intelligible—but not self-evident. There are laws, but also gaps. Patterns, but also exceptions. What we see is form with room in it—a world that coheres just enough to be studied, but not so completely as to be closed.

This tension has long shaped philosophical and scientific thought. The cosmos behaves in ways that allow prediction, theory, and engineering. Yet its foundations remain opaque. We have no final theory. No unbroken chain of explanation. We know how gravity bends light, but not why the gravitational constant has the value it does. We know how particles interact, but not what breathes possibility into the field they arise from.

There is coherence—but also strangeness. Law—but not finality. We live in a universe that invites understanding, while withholding its full origin. That feels designed for inquiry, but not resolved for comfort.

Some have taken this tension as evidence of fine-tuning. Others have taken it as proof of randomness. But perhaps it is something else entirely: a reflection of what happens when form emerges without direction, when pattern arises without a goal, and logic appears only after being stabilizes.

If that's the case, then the world is not a finished system. It is a settled turbulence—a balance between design and possibility. A world that holds together, but does not explain itself.

That's not a flaw. It may be the very condition for experience. If the universe were maximally ordered, it might leave no room for freedom, creativity, or thought. If it were fully random, nothing would endure. But this—this world of half-lit patterns and nearly stable laws—allows for everything we know.

It allows for error. For imagination. For science. For loss.

It allows for life.

What Emergence Might Really Mean

Emergence is a word that often promises more than it explains. We use it to describe how complexity arises from simplicity, how coherence seems to surface without being imposed. In science, it's applied to everything from the formation of galaxies to the flocking of birds, from traffic patterns to the possible unfolding of consciousness from physical substrates. But in all these cases, emergence takes place within systems—networks of material, energy, or interaction governed by laws.

The kind of emergence we're asking about is different. We're not speaking of behavior that unfolds within a structure. We're asking about emergence before there was structure. Before there were laws, fields, relations. No spacetime. No logic. No direction. Just being, arising from absolute nothingness—an unformed presence, appearing where there had been no framework at all—and then somehow beginning to take shape.

So what could emergence mean in that context?

Perhaps it begins with distinction. The moment anything exists, even in the smallest possible sense, there is a difference: this, not that; here, not elsewhere. To exist is to be distinct—even if only from the nothing that preceded it. And once distinction exists, relation follows. With relation comes contrast. With contrast, the possibility of repetition, and from repetition, the earliest forms of pattern.

Order may not require design. It may arise simply because being, once it exists, begins to echo itself. Not intentionally, not with aim, but because presence interacts. It folds, reflects, interferes. And in that interaction, form appears—not by blueprint, but by recurrence. Not because it was destined, but because it endures. Regularities that persist outlast those that fall apart. And over time, what holds becomes what is.

In this view, mathematics is not a code written before the world. It is a language the world teaches itself. Logic is not a law the universe follows. It is a rhythm the universe learns to speak. Order is not the plan of being—it is how being begins to stabilize.

This is not a romantic picture. There is no secret intelligence behind it. No perfection. No arc. Just the quiet unfolding of pattern from the bare fact of presence.

If emergence means anything here, it means this: once something exists, relation is unavoidable, and from relation, pattern can grow. Emergence is not an added layer. It is how being begins to shape itself.

If mathematics and logic arose with being—if they were not prewritten into the void, but arose from relation and contrast—then the foundations of structure are themselves ungrounded. They did not precede reality. They formed within it.

If even our clearest principles arise after the fact, then the universe may rest on no bedrock at all—only on what manages, moment by moment, to continue holding.

And that leads us to the next layer of the question: What about the laws of physics?

Not the abstractions of number or the logic of form, but the specific regularities that govern this world—the spin of particles, the pull of gravity, the expansion of space, the constancy of light. These laws give the universe its texture. They are what make phenomena repeatable, matter stable, time measurable. They offer coherence—not just to thought, but to existence.

But are they necessary? Could the laws of physics have arisen just as spontaneously as pattern—settling into place not by choice or design, but because they were simply stable enough to last once being began?

In other words, is it possible for a universe like ours to hold together without foundations?

That is where the ground begins to give way.

CHAPTER 5

When Foundations Disappear

*How Physics Replaced Metaphysics—and Then Shattered
Its Own Foundations*

P hysics, as we know it today, was born in defiance—though not
in complete severance from all metaphysical commitments.
It emerged not as a continuation of Aristotelian and scholastic
metaphysics, but as their rebellion. The early architects of modern science—Galileo, Descartes, Newton—sought to strip the world of its hidden purposes, divine causes, and layered meanings. In their place, they
offered a cleaner vocabulary: motion, mass, force, time. Their project was
not just empirical but philosophical. It aimed to reframe the idea of explanation—not as the unveiling of final causes, but as the identification
of invariant laws.

This shift did not happen all at once. For centuries, physics had been
nested within metaphysics. Aristotle's physics was inseparable from his account of form and purpose. Motion was not just change, but the fulfillment
of a thing's nature. The heavens moved not only by geometry but by being
moved through desire for the unmoved mover—drawn toward pure actu-
ality. Even in the medieval world, where theology reigned, metaphysical
structure was presumed to underlie natural phenomena. To explain the
world was to situate it within a broader logic of creation.

But with the rise of modern science, these assumptions were suspended.
The new physics no longer asked why bodies fell, but how. It did not seek

the meaning of planetary motion, but its equation. The success of this method was astonishing—and seductive. Metaphysics, with all its speculative scaffolding, seemed suddenly unnecessary. The world, it appeared, could be described in terms of quantity, not quality. Structure could be mapped without appealing to essence. Law could replace purpose.

From the beginning, this victory came with a paradox. In stripping away metaphysics, physics had quietly borrowed from it. The laws of motion, the fabric of space, the constancy of time—these were treated as given. They were not explained but assumed. The world behaved mathematically, and this fact was treated as fundamental. But why should it? Why should matter obey order? Why should there be structure at all?

This was the tension buried beneath the triumph. For all its explanatory power, physics had smuggled in its own presuppositions—forms of regularity, causality, and coherence that had no physical cause. It had exiled metaphysical speculation only to inherit its unresolved foundations. And as the centuries passed, these foundations would begin to shake.

The early foundations held for a time. Newtonian mechanics, with its absolute space, uniform time, and deterministic laws, seemed to offer a stable scaffold for the world. Everything moved according to principle. Cause led to effect. The future, if not yet known, was already written in the language of mass and force—commitments Newton believed were sustained by divine providence. But this sense of foundation began to crack in the twentieth century.

Einstein's relativity altered more than our measurements of space and time—it undermined their status as fixed backgrounds. Space could bend. Time could stretch. The geometry of the universe was not imposed upon it from above but shaped by what it contained. Suddenly, structure was not a stage but a consequence. The cosmos did not unfold within a fixed arena. It sculpted its own arena as it went.

Quantum theory took this unraveling further. At microscopic scales, certainty gave way to probability. The sharp predictability of classical mechanics dissolved into a haze of potential states. In the Copenhagen interpretation, a quantum system exists only as a spread of possibilities until an interaction with the world forces one to become real—in this view, measurement itself seems to take part in what emerges, though other interpretations dispute this. And the deeper physicists dug, the stranger the ground became. Particles behaved like waves. Identity blurred. Events appeared to lack definite cause until measured. The very act of trying to describe what was there changed what was there.

These were not just technical puzzles. They challenged the idea that physics rested on solid foundations. If the geometry of space could flex, if time could dilate, if measurement could shape what is real—then what, exactly, was fundamental? What lay beneath the equations? Were the laws themselves fixed and eternal, or did they emerge along with the universe they described?

The search for certainty began to feel like a mirage. Each layer of explanation opened onto another, until even the idea of a final foundation started to feel like a holdover from an older metaphysics. The world was not built atop bedrock, but nested within riddles. The equations worked, and yet the meanings of their terms kept dissolving under scrutiny. Space, time, mass, energy—none remained untouched.

In this light, physics did not so much eliminate metaphysics as inherit its crisis. The structure of the world could no longer be treated as obvious, given, or prior. Even the idea of law—once the anchor of natural order—began to seem like a feature of the system rather than its cause. The very notion of foundation had slipped.

Is Law Itself Emergent?

For centuries, the laws of nature were treated as eternal. Even as metaphysical scaffolding fell away, the idea of fixed, universal law remained intact. Gravity, electromagnetism, thermodynamics—these principles seemed not just stable, but fundamental. They structured the cosmos. They explained the dance of planets, the behavior of gases, the curvature of light. If the universe was a machine, these were its rules.

But what if the rules have a history?

This possibility has gained traction—not as speculative philosophy, but as a serious scientific proposal. In cosmology and theoretical physics, some now suggest that physical laws may not be timeless fixtures, but emergent features. They may evolve. They may crystallize under specific conditions. They may even fluctuate at the far edges of the universe or in its earliest moments. In this view, law is not the precondition of the universe but its consequence.

Several developments point in this direction. In the early universe, for example, symmetry breaking is thought—according to the standard model of cosmology—to have led to the emergence of distinct forces. What began as a unified field fractured into gravity, electromagnetism, and the nuclear forces. The constants that govern their behavior—the charge of the electron, the strength of the strong force—are thought to have settled into their current values only after the universe cooled. These parameters were not fixed in advance. They arose as the system unfolded.

Some theorists have extended this logic further. Perhaps even the laws we consider universal are effective laws—stable approximations that hold only under certain conditions, much like the behavior of waves in water. The rules emerge from the medium. Change the medium, and the rules change. In such a framework, the laws of nature are not written into the substrate of being. They are epiphenomena—patterns that arise from deeper, possibly shifting, levels of structure.

But if laws emerge from deeper conditions, then their authority is not absolute. They describe what happens here, under these constraints, with these values—not what must happen everywhere. Their regularity becomes local, contextual, dependent on the unfolding of the system itself. This is a different kind of order. Not the kind we imagine as timeless or inviolate, but the kind that crystallizes—stable enough to function, yet possibly fragile at its edges. In this view, what we call a "law" is less a cosmic mandate than a persistent habit of being. And that habit may not extend indefinitely.

This does not make them meaningless. It makes them contingent.

And if law is contingent, then the bedrock of explanation has shifted. We can no longer treat the equations of physics as givens. We must ask what makes law possible in the first place. What generates the conditions under which stable order can arise? What allows pattern to persist? These are not questions physics is well-equipped to answer, because they precede the domain in which physics operates.

The idea that law is emergent returns us to a deeper uncertainty. For if the rules are not eternal, then what accounts for their appearance? Why does anything behave in a regular way at all?

Perhaps the deeper miracle is not that the universe obeys law—but that it coheres long enough for law to be inferred.

Order Without Law?

The idea that law may be emergent is unsettling, but it still leaves open the possibility that law-like behavior can be grounded in something deeper—a meta-structure, a statistical necessity, a pattern in the chaos. But what if we go further? What if even this is too much? What if we ask not how law arises from being, but how order arises without law?

This question pushes the boundaries of what explanation usually permits. It strips away not only rule but regularity. It asks how coherence can emerge from incoherence, how constraint can arise where nothing constrains. And it brings us face to face with a kind of metaphysical vertigo. Because if there is no prior law—no principle, no geometry, no tendency—then we are no longer explaining order by appeal to what precedes it. We are watching it happen in real time, from nothing.

Some models in physics already lean toward this. In the study of complex systems, it is well known that local randomness can give rise to global patterns. Order can emerge from fluctuation. In certain cellular automata, a simple rule applied to random inputs can yield intricate, structured outputs—grids that resemble snowflakes, spirals, or even computation. These results depend not on fine-tuned inputs but on the self-organizing potential of the system itself.

But even here, the rules are predefined. The system operates within a fixed frame. What would it mean to imagine a system where even the rules were not given? Where structure appears without the aid of background instruction?

Here, we move beyond established physics into metaphysical speculation. This is the frontier at which metaphysics returns—not in the form of dogma or doctrine, but as the unavoidable horizon of intelligibility. Physics can describe emergence. It can model how systems evolve under constraints. But it cannot fully account for the appearance of the constraints themselves, if they are not already latent in the structure of reality. If law is not prior, and pattern is not programmed, then we are forced to confront a scenario in which being self-organizes without instruction.

That idea is not only difficult. It is radical. Because it means that order is not inherited—it is born.

If order is born rather than inherited, then the very idea of understanding may need to shift. Explanation has always rested on the hope of reduction—that patterns can be traced to rules, rules to principles, principles to something deeper. But if nothing lies beneath, if pattern is primary and law is a latecomer, then explanation becomes description. Science still works—but it maps what is, not what must be. This isn't the collapse of intelligibility. It's the end of foundationalism. It means we live in a universe that makes sense in places, but not because it was built to be coherent. Coherence may simply be what survives.

That's not disorder. But it's not grounding, either.

The End of Foundations

We began this chapter with the premise that physics emerged in rebellion against metaphysics. But by tracing its trajectory, we've seen that this rebellion was incomplete. For all its explanatory success, physics never fully escaped the metaphysical ground it sought to erase. It displaced one kind of foundation—final causes, divine intention, cosmic hierarchy—only to assume another. Law replaced purpose. Structure replaced essence. But the idea that there is something stable beneath what appears never fully disappeared.

Now even that assumption is under pressure.

If the laws of nature are not fixed, if order can emerge without prior rules, then there may be no foundation in the traditional sense at all. Not in metaphysics. Not in physics. Not in logic, mathematics, or symmetry. Each of these once promised a grounding. But each now appears vulnerable to the same question: what makes it possible? And beneath that, what makes anything possible?

The temptation is to rebuild—quickly, cleanly, and with new materials. To invoke *the anthropic principle*—the idea that the universe's laws seem tuned to us because only in such a world could we appear; *the multiverse*—the imagined sweep of countless universes, each with its own design; *informational compression*—the thought that immense complexity might flow from hidden, simple rules; or *simulation theory*—the proposal that reality itself is the work of an unseen architect. All of them remain speculative proposals. To imagine some deeper pattern that explains the patterns. But each of these explanations presumes something rather than nothing. Each invokes a structure to explain structure, a form to justify form. And so we return, not to an answer, but to the absence we began with.

This absence is not a gap to be filled. It is the condition we must think from.

We are no longer asking what underlies the universe. We are asking what it means for a universe to arise without anything to underlie it. A universe without fixed law, without eternal principle, without even the scaffolding of logic. If such a thing is possible, then being is not the result of a system. It is the appearance of coherence where no coherence was required.

The foundations did not hold. And still, being appeared.

CHAPTER 6

When Being Becomes Aware

Why Consciousness Can't Be Explained

O f all the things that exist, consciousness is the most immediate and the most mysterious. It's not distant, not abstract, not something inferred. It is what we are. Every thought, every doubt, every act of inquiry happens within it. And yet, for all its closeness, consciousness resists every attempt to explain it. The more we try to locate it in the world, the more it slips through the fingers of theory. It is at once ordinary and uncanny, intimate and strange.

Here the concern is with the felt, subjective side of experience—the felt reality of being aware, here and now. This is sometimes called phenomenal consciousness. It is not just the ability to notice, report, or act on information. It is the presence of experience itself.

The prevailing view in much of philosophy and neuroscience is that consciousness "emerges" from complex arrangements of matter. On this view, it is not a basic feature of reality; it is a byproduct. The brain reaches a certain level of complexity—neurons fire, networks form, information integrates—and somehow, awareness appears.

But what kind of "emergence" could this be? In science, emergence often refers to new properties that show up when parts interact in certain ways. The liquidity of water is not obvious from the behavior of isolated hydrogen and oxygen atoms. The flight of a bird is not fully explained by the properties of feathers or wings. Yet in these cases, the new property—liquidity, flight—remains physical. Nothing radically new has been introduced.

Consciousness is different. It does not merely behave in unexpected ways—it opens a realm apart: the distance between motion and meaning, between structure and experience. Everything else can be spoken of in terms of what it does; consciousness also carries the fact of what it is like to be. One could trace the movements of matter through infinite detail and still never touch the simple, impossible truth that anything is being felt.

This is the "hard problem" of consciousness: not how the brain processes information, but how subjective experience arises at all. Why should any physical system, no matter how complex, give rise to a point of view? Why should there be something it is like to be that system?

No description of structure, function, or mechanism—no matter how detailed—appears capable of generating the presence of experience from purely structural facts. If emergence is to explain this, it must show how being becomes aware of itself. And that seems to be more than emergence can carry.

The Point Where Explanation Fails

Materialism—the view that everything real is ultimately physical—has been enormously successful. Physics, chemistry, and biology have each advanced by explaining phenomena in terms of matter, energy, and their interactions. The mind, from this perspective, is no exception. It is what the brain does. Thought is computation. Emotion is chemistry. Consciousness, too, should be a process that can, in principle, be mapped, measured, and explained.

Reductionism sharpened this claim, holding that higher-level phenomena are nothing over and above their parts. A storm is air in motion. A gene is a sequence of nucleotides. A mind is a pattern of neuronal activity. Understand the parts and their interactions, and the whole is explained. Nothing remains.

But with consciousness, something remains. One can describe every synapse, every chemical signal in the brain—and still not reach the fact of what it is like to feel pain, to see red, to remember a face that matters. These *qualia*—the felt qualities of experience—are not behaviors or functions. They are not outputs. They are lived.

Functionalism tried a different approach, shifting the focus from what a system is made of to what it does. If something performs the same operations as a conscious brain, perhaps it is conscious too. This allows for the idea that consciousness is like software that could run on different hardware.

But the problem persists. Two systems could behave identically, and one might still be "dark inside"—no one home. Philosophers debate whether imagining such "zombie" systems proves they are possible, but even if they are only conceivable, that alone marks a conceptual gap any structural account must still bridge.

This is the heart of the mystery. No account of structure or function explains how experience enters the picture. Not the content of experience, but the fact of its existence at all. That the world is revealed from within. This is not hidden—it is the most obvious fact of our lives. And yet it remains untouched by explanation.

Responses to the Hard Problem

Many approaches have been tried. One is *illusionism*: the claim that consciousness is not what it seems, and that the sense of having a private inner life is a kind of trick. On this view, there are no experiences—only brain processes that make it seem as if there are. Pain is not felt. Red is not seen. The brain simply behaves as if it were.

The difficulty is that illusions are themselves experienced. To deny experience is to use the very thing one is denying. Illusionism may protect a certain view of the physical world, but it does so by discarding the phenomenon it was meant to explain.

Others expand the picture. *Panpsychism* says consciousness is basic and exists in some form at every level of reality. This avoids the puzzle of how awareness could suddenly appear in complex brains if it is nowhere in the parts. But it raises another challenge: how do tiny fragments of awareness combine into the unified experience we know? Some panpsychists answer with "field" or "cosmopsychist" models, where unity is primary and parts are derivative. Yet even then, there is the question of why certain local structures would host intense, coherent experience while others would not.

Dualism holds that mind and matter are fundamentally different. From this standpoint, consciousness does not arise from the brain at all—it is something else, joined to the body. This avoids reducing mind to matter, but creates its own problems: how could two different kinds of thing inter-act, and why would they be connected at all?

Idealism turns the usual order upside-down, saying consciousness is primary and the physical world arises within it. This is bold, but difficult to formulate clearly and harder still to test.

A further group of views—non-reductive physicalism, which holds that consciousness is real yet cannot be collapsed into pure physics; Russellian monism, which sees matter as carrying hidden properties hospitable to ex-perience; and neutral monism, which understands mind and matter as two faces of a deeper common reality—keeps the physical world fundamental but says it must have intrinsic properties capable of realizing experience. This overlaps with the position taken here to the extent that it puts pres-ence "in the base." The difference is that such presence is not inferred from structure—it is known directly in experience.

Each of these approaches tries, in its own way, to close the gap be-tween mechanism and experience. None fully succeeds. Either they deny what seems undeniable, or they posit entities and properties that cannot be observed, combined, or reconciled with the rest of what is known. The problem remains.

Experience and the Question of Ground

If none of these explanations succeed—if they cannot show how awareness could arise from structure—then we are left with a deeper question: what makes anything appear at all?

Earlier chapters asked how structure could emerge from nothing, how law could arise without being fixed, how pattern could form without being compelled. Consciousness joins this list—not as an exception, but as another case in which appearance cannot be traced to a prior source.

Even the boldest theories of mind point to patterns, functions, systems—forms of order. They assume the right kind of order will give rise to experience. But why should it? The principle at work here is simple: if basic reality gives only structure—relations and arrangements—it cannot produce intrinsic presence out of nothing. Presence must already be in the base, or the base must be expanded.

We do not know why coherence leads to awareness. We do not know what makes any system capable of feeling, even in the smallest degree. We only know that it happens. And if there is no fixed law, no eternal structure, no hidden store of potential, then it cannot be traced to anything deeper.

Consciousness appears not because it was required, encoded, or inevitable. It appears because being itself can become aware.

If consciousness cannot be reduced, explained away, or built out of structure alone, then what remains is extraordinary: the presence of experience where no experience was required. A phenomenon that arrives uninvited, that cannot be explained from below, and that reveals the world from within.

This is not just a failure of explanation. It is a clue.

It suggests that awareness does not fit into current models—not because it is too complex, but because it is a different kind of reality. It does not arise from the machinery of the world; it discloses it. It opens a point of view, a center of perspective, a field in which anything can appear.

We have reached the edge of emergence. Here there is a hint of similar limits in explaining physics, law, and order—but those belong to later chapters. At some point there is no "before" to appeal to. There is only appearance—only the eruption of what was not there a moment before.

This does not mean there is a cause we have not yet found. It means the kind of cause we are looking for may not exist.

And so we arrive at a threshold. If consciousness cannot be reduced to structure, if law cannot be grounded in form, if being cannot be traced to anything deeper—then we are not looking at a system. We are facing something else. Something that comes not from beneath, but from beyond.

A light with no source—no source, at least, within the structural frame of the world we can describe.

And if the light of consciousness cannot be accounted for from within the structure itself, then we are pressed to consider other possibilities. One of these, taken up in the next chapter, is that being may not just appear—it may be given. And if it is given, then perhaps consciousness is not an accident at all, but part of what giving makes possible.

Between Emergence and Intention

When Emergence and Intention Are Seen as Complementary, Not Opposed

We are not abandoning the previous path. We are stepping beside it. The exploration of emergence has carried us to the edge of what can be said about order without origin, coherence without law, awareness without prior cause. That path remains open, unclosed. Yet before turning to the possibility of intention, it is worth asking whether these accounts must stand as rivals at all. Perhaps they can be read not as competing claims, but as perspectives that reveal different dimensions of the same mystery.

Emergence, as we have traced it, is a story of process. It shows how coherence can arise in the absence of scaffolding, how patterns may crystallize out of instability, how order can appear where nothing compels it. Intention, by contrast, is not a mechanism but a ground. It is the suggestion that being itself is not an accident of collapse, but the result of a choice—or at least of a will that does not allow absolute absence to prevail. The one describes how coherence unfolds; the other opens onto why there is anything at all for coherence to inhabit.

There is no need to collapse one into the other. To speak of intention is not to deny the real power of emergence. It does not erase the picture of a universe flowering from instability, or diminish the beauty of coherence that requires no hand to draw its lines. It simply suggests that beneath the unfolding there may be a deeper permission, a silent ground that allows the unfolding to occur. Intention here is not a rival explanation but a foundation beneath explanation itself.

Seen in this way, the two paths are not contradictory but layered. Imagine a canvas and a painting: the surface provides the condition for form, but the strokes are free to move in directions not predetermined by the ground beneath them. Emergence may be the paint, full of dynamism and surprise; intention may be the unspoken allowance that there is a canvas at all. The picture that results is not imposed from without, but neither is it without a ground that makes its appearance possible.

Philosophy has long been tempted to force a choice between such accounts. Either coherence is self-generated, arising through lawless instability, or it is imposed by a mind, a will, a principle of design. Yet perhaps this opposition is too stark. A more subtle reading sees them as addressing different questions. Emergence speaks to the dynamics of unfolding within being; intention speaks to the possibility of being itself. They are not two answers to the same puzzle but two dimensions of the same mystery.

This dual vision also guards against the dangers of reduction. If we hold only to emergence, we risk leaving the "why" unanswered, imagining that description of process suffices for the question of existence. If we hold only to intention, we risk imagining a fixed decree, a rigid determination that leaves no room for novelty or openness. Taken together, the two perspectives preserve both the freedom of becoming and the depth of origin. They allow us to imagine a universe that is both gift and unfolding, both permitted and uncoerced.

The bridge, then, is not a compromise but an opening. Emergence may describe how the world develops—how order, life, and awareness arise where none were before. Intention may address why such development occurs at all, why there is something to unfold rather than silence. They may belong together, intention as the depth that allows unfolding and emergence as the shape it takes. Or they may stand apart, each offering its own account of origin. In either case, to move from one to the other is not to abandon a path but to widen it, to recognize that the mystery of being may be more spacious than any single explanation can contain.

PART III
Theories of Intention

From Emergence to Intention

We now move into another way of seeing. The way forward admits more than one possibility. Emergence alone may account for being from nothing, as coherence arises unbidden from instability. Intention alone may account for it, as existence is given rather than accidental. Or the two may belong together—emergence tracing the shape of unfolding, intention naming the source that lets it begin. However conceived—separately or together—intention shifts the question. It turns from the pattern of appearance to the fact of appearance itself.

> *"Not how the world is, but that it is, is the mystical."*
> —LUDWIG WITTGENSTEIN, *TRACTATUS LOGICO-PHILOSOPHICUS*

The previous chapters explored the possibility that order, law, and the light of consciousness arose spontaneously—from nothing, without plan or purpose. We followed each of these to the edge of emergence, where structure appears unbidden, coherence arrives without cause, and awareness stands as a presence that structure alone cannot explain. But what if that is not the whole story? What if the appearance of being is not an accident, but an act—not random, but willed?

This part of the book turns to that question. Not to answer it, but to open it. To explore what it might mean to say that being was chosen—not by a force within the system, but by a source beyond it. A source not outside the universe, but outside of all structure, all form, all logic, all time. If being arose from true nothingness, then any intention behind it cannot belong to being. It must come from beyond space and time, beyond causality and consciousness, beyond even the possibility of structure. Not earlier, not elsewhere— but radically other. Not outside of what is, but outside of what could be.

It is natural to wonder whether speaking of "intention" at all undermines the very idea of absolute nothingness. If intention brought being into existence, does that not make intention itself a "something"—and thus mean that nothingness was never truly nothing? The account explored here takes that concern seriously. It treats intention not as an entity, process, or latent potential, but as wholly outside the scope of what can be called "something" or "nothing." In this framing, intention is not a member of reality; it is not even a possibility within the void. It is that which stands beyond both, such that its presence does not break the condition of nothingness because it does not exist *in* or *as* that condition at all.

The next chapter will take this question head-on, showing why intention—properly understood—does not violate the idea of radical nothingness but depends upon it.

For intention to be metaphysically coherent in the context of absolute nothingness, it must originate from outside every category that being contains.

This is not a return to doctrine or design. It is not a gesture toward mythology or metaphysical comfort. It is an attempt to think from another dimension—from the possibility that what exists does so because it was meant to, even if the nature of that meaning remains hidden. Intention, in this sense, is not a conclusion. It is a different kind of beginning. It asks not only how the world came to be, but why freedom might have been part of that becoming. It allows us to consider whether concealment is not the absence of meaning, but the condition in which meaning, belief, and even goodness become possible.

To ask whether being was intended is to ask whether reality carries a bias toward appearance—whether something gave itself without being compelled, without being bound, without being anything we can recognize. The chapters that follow do not seek to prove this. They seek to hold the question open. Because if emergence reveals what can unfold when nothing cannot hold, then intention suggests what might arise when being is given—not because nothing fails, but because something wills.

CHAPTER 7

When Being Is a Gift

The Possibility That Existence Was Willed, Not Forced

W e have reached the edge of one story. The previous chapters followed a path of emergence: the idea that structure, order, and even consciousness could arise without plan, from nothing, through instability or spontaneous coherence. It was a path that resisted traditional metaphysics, rejected necessity, and asked whether law could simply appear. But we have now traced that path to its limit. And at that limit, something remains unanswered—not a detail or mechanism, but the question of why anything should appear at all.

It is the question that sits beneath every other. To say that coherence emerged is to describe a pattern, but it does not explain its possibility. Why should there be order in the absence of law? Why should structure arise where no principle required it? Why should awareness appear where no system predicted it? Each of these may be framed as a scientific puzzle, but beneath the puzzle lies a deeper pressure: what if being itself was not only unopposed, but given—granted not in time, as an event among events, but in a sense outside any before or after? And if so, is such a world necessary, contingent, or of a kind that escapes both categories? The answer here leans toward the last—neither bound by necessity nor dependent on chance in the usual sense.

This is not a return to myth or doctrine. It is not an appeal to creation in the theological sense. The hypothesis we now approach is more difficult. It suggests that existence may not be accidental—that it may be an act, not a consequence. Not inevitable. Not imposed. Not derived from law. But willed—and here "willed" means something analogical: a fundamental leaning toward expression, not a deliberation or plan in the human sense. If a "reason" is sought for such willing, it would not be a cause in time, but the willing itself as a primitive ground—an answer that does not defer to anything deeper.

That possibility requires us to shift our mode of questioning. It is no longer enough to ask how order arose. We must ask what kind of reality would will it. What would it mean for being to be chosen? What would it mean for nothing to give way, not under pressure, but in freedom?

What Would It Mean for Being to Be Chosen?

To speak of being as chosen is to move beyond emergence. Not to deny it, but to step behind it—to ask whether the appearance of order, form, and experience might reflect not an accident, but an act.

And not an act in the ordinary sense. There was no hand, no voice, no agent among other agents. There was nothing. And then, inexplicably, there was something (here "then" is only a figure of speech; no time passed in the source itself).

But if something willed being into existence, it could not have belonged to being, nor could it have been part of nothingness as a latent possibility. If it were a latent possibility, then nothingness would already contain a form of being—contradicting the very definition of radical nothingness on which this account depends.

It is better understood as a boundary—the point where our usual ways of thinking no longer work. Like treating the horizon as an object sitting on the horizon, when in fact it is the limit of sight itself. In this sense, "intention" does not exist as a feature within reality, nor as a hidden structure in the void—it names the possibility that the transition from absence to presence was allowed, yet without that allowance existing as part of either pole.

To speak of what lies outside both something and nothing is not to introduce a third category, as though there were a hidden domain beyond them. It is to point toward the collapse of all categories at the outer edge of thought. Here, even the distinction between being and non-being no longer applies. We must speak in metaphors because no literal description is possible; but the metaphors are scaffolding, not structure—provisional aids to thought that must be set aside once they have done their work.

It may still feel, even after this, as though such intention must exist somewhere—perhaps not within our universe, but in some other realm. This is a reflex of thought, not a truth about the idea itself. 'Somewhere' is already part of being; it is a category whose meaning depends entirely on being, and so could not apply before being itself appeared. Intention in this sense has no location. It does not occupy a space beyond the universe, nor is it hidden within some parallel order. It is more like the condition for location itself—the silent backdrop against which both 'something' and 'nothing' appear. To treat it as an existent is to mistake the frame for the picture, or to think of zero as a number one might physically encounter in the world.

It must be beyond structure, beyond contrast, beyond even the possibility of relation. Whatever it was, it cannot be part of the story it began. But if that transition was not driven by necessity, nor produced by instability, then what remains is the idea of willing—an impulse that cannot be reduced to process.

This is not the will of deliberation or calculation, nor the human will shaped by motive or constraint. It is something more elemental: a willing that comes before cause, a letting-be that allows form to arise without requiring a reason. Here "letting-be" refers to a grounding relation rather than an event—language borrowed only because there are no direct terms for such a source.

We have no language for this. Every metaphor bends back toward the familiar. We imagine a choice, and we imagine a chooser. We reach for terms like mind, creator, agent. But each of these carries associations we do not intend—too shaped by narrative, too full of personality, too embedded in time. Such projections are not harmless analogies; they import the very structures—time, form, subject—that this account seeks to leave behind.

And yet the intuition persists: that what is might have been, in some deep sense, wanted.

Not in the way that plans are made or purposes assigned, but as an ontological affirmation. Not this instead of that, but something instead of nothing. A movement not toward utility or outcome, but toward manifestation itself.

This would not explain being. It would not solve the mystery. It would deepen it. But it would reframe the mystery not as a rupture, nor as a chance event, but as an expression. Not a consequence of laws, but the arrival of presence through something more like volition—something that gives rise without being made to do so.

If emergence is what happens when nothing cannot hold, then intention is what happens when being is given—not because nothing fails, but because something wills. And while some might see such 'willing' as a poetic way of describing a cosmic disposition, it would instead be a foundation for being, not a tendency contained within being.

It would be the reason there is any reason at all.

Intention Without a Who

The moment we speak of intention, a figure begins to form. We imagine a mind, a presence, a chooser. Someone who wills. Someone who acts. This image arrives unbidden—shaped by centuries of mythology, religion, and personal projection. But it may not belong here. If we are asking whether being was chosen, we must also ask whether intention requires a self.

We are accustomed to thinking of intention as psychological. It involves awareness, desire, deliberation. A subject stands apart from its world, considers alternatives, selects a path. But that model presumes complexity, temporality, and embodiment. It presumes a world already in place. And we are not talking about that kind of world. We are asking whether the first gesture—the appearance of anything at all—might have been expressive, not automatic. A letting-be, not a result.

Such an unfolding need not belong to someone. It need not arise from agency in the familiar sense. It may be closer to what we find in art than in design: the first stroke of a brush—prior to goal, plan, or self-conscious-ness. A movement of giving rather than acquiring. A becoming that is not decided upon, but flowing from a depth beyond words.

In this framing, intention is not a decision made by something that already is. It is more like the condition under which being can appear with-out being compelled—an opening that is not itself part of what it opens. In that sense, intention functions as a boundary concept—a marker for where explanation reaches the edge of what can be said, without crossing into what can be described as either something or nothing.

This is not an attempt to revive the idea of a divine personality. It is not a rebranding of theism. It is something less certain and more difficult: the possibility that reality bears a bias toward expression—not because it has a reason, but because it does not require one. This would not be a mind that plans. It would not be a will that intervenes. It would be a source without subject, an intention without a who.

That phrase may be hard to hold. It unravels under the weight of lan-guage. But it points toward something just beyond the reach of explana-tion—a movement toward the possibility that being does not simply exist, but offers itself, without identity, without calculation, without origin in anything other than itself.

The Risks and Consequences of Intention

To suggest that being was chosen—however abstractly—is to open the door to meaning. Not imposed meaning, not a scripted purpose, but mean-ing in the deepest sense: the idea that existence is not arbitrary. That what is, in some hidden way, matters.

And yet this suggestion brings with it a burden. Because once we begin to imagine that being was willed, we must also ask: why this being? Why this world, with all its beauty and its pain?

This is where the hypothesis of intention encounters its most seri-ous challenge. If reality was chosen, then suffering was not permitted by randomness. It was, in some sense, allowed by will. If coherence was desired, then so was its fragility. And if experience was given, then so were limits, loss, and death.

These consequences cannot be ignored. They weigh heavily on any picture of metaphysical intention.

Because if being was willed—even in the most abstract, impersonal sense—then the world is not only allowed, but welcomed. And that means all of it: the beauty and the terror, the ache of grief and the joy of form. Pain, in this light, is no longer meaningless—but neither is it justified. It simply exists alongside every other facet of experience, inseparable from the gift.

This is not an argument for comfort. It is a confrontation with cost. To imagine that being was chosen is to accept that what we live was not permitted by chance, but borne—intentionally, though not necessarily with purpose.

That is a heavier view, not a lighter one. It demands not belief, but humility.

Humility is the only posture wide enough to hold it.

One possible reason for such a world is that freedom and certain goods—love, courage, fidelity—require vulnerability and cannot exist without the possibility of loss. If the source is non-coercive, risk may be built into the very conditions of expression. And if this is so, then concealment may serve a similar purpose: a world without overt signs of its source would be one in which trust, discovery, and self-chosen commitments are possible.

There is also the problem of concealment. If being was chosen, why does that choosing leave no obvious trace? Why does the universe appear self-sufficient, indifferent, unmarked by signature or design? If intention is real, it is the quietest kind. It does not announce itself. It does not demand belief. It leaves everything in place, including doubt—perhaps because such silence is the only way for meaning to arise without imposition.

Silence may be the last gift of a giving that does not take back.

From Emergence to Intention

The idea that being was chosen is not a conclusion. It is not a solution to the mystery of existence, nor a replacement for the accounts we have already considered. It is a shift in stance—a reorientation of thought that begins where the language of emergence can no longer reach.

If emergence describes what happens when nothing gives way under pressure, then intention imagines what happens when nothing gives way freely. Where one posits instability, the other suggests expression. Where one sees order as a product, the other sees it as an offering.

We are not abandoning the previous path. We are stepping beside it. The possibility of intention does not deny that coherence can arise without cause. It does not dispute that patterns can form in the absence of law. Indeed, the two accounts may be layered—intention as the atemporal ground, emergence as the mode through which being unfolds.

In this sense, the bridge remains open: emergence may describe how being develops, while intention speaks to why it appears at all.

The next chapters explore this possibility. Not with answers, but with care. We will consider whether mind might precede matter, whether the source of being might remain hidden, and whether the universe allows meaning without imposition. These are not doctrinal inquiries. They are philosophical invitations. They arise not from certainty, but from the silence left by every other attempt to explain why there is something rather than nothing.

If emergence showed us what reality can do without guidance, intention asks what it might mean for reality to be guided—gently, silently, and without force.

CHAPTER 8

When Mind Comes First

Awareness as the Basis of Reality

For most of human history, it was taken for granted that mind came first. In one form or another, this was the prevailing intuition: that reality was shaped, permeated, or upheld by some form of intelligence. The ancient philosophers spoke of *Nous*—mind—and *Logos*—reason, or the principle of order—as the deep grammar of existence. In many spiritual traditions, the world was not a mute object but a disclosure, something spoken, dreamed, or thought into being. Even in the early sciences, there lingered the sense that nature was intelligible because it had been ordered by more than chance.

This orientation did not always mean belief in a personal deity. Often, it was more abstract: a sense that form, meaning, or presence required some underlying principle of mind. Matter, in this view, was not self-explanatory. It needed something prior—something that gave it structure, coherence, or direction. The world appeared not as brute fact, but as manifestation.

Only in the modern era did this assumption begin to reverse. With the rise of mechanistic science, mind was gradually relocated. It became an afterthought, a feature of certain animals, a side effect of brains. The prevailing view came to be that matter is fundamental, and mind is something it produces. Thought is chemistry. Consciousness is computation. Experience is what happens when matter becomes complex enough to simulate itself.

This reversal proved immensely productive. It allowed science to disentangle itself from metaphysics and to describe the world with astonishing precision. Yet the question remains: did it go too far? In explaining everything from the outside, have we forgotten that for anything to appear at all, it must also be revealed from within?

That is the tension now under reconsideration. The idea that mind might be primary is no longer fashionable, but it may not be obsolete. It may have been set aside not because it was answered, but because it was deferred. Having followed matter to its furthest edge, we can once again ask—not whether mind emerged from matter, but whether matter is the appearance of mind. Here, "mind" refers not to a personal thinker with goals, but to an intrinsic, non-deliberative basis for appearance itself.

The Limits of Physicalism

The modern view of consciousness begins with the assumption that everything real is, in some final sense, physical. At its foundation, this is the claim of physicalism: that all phenomena—experience included—can ultimately be explained in terms of matter, energy, and the laws that govern them. Mind, within this framework, is not an independent feature of the universe, but a product of physical processes. The brain gives rise to awareness in the way a furnace gives rise to heat, or a circuit gives rise to light.

This account has the advantage of simplicity. It places everything on a single explanatory plane. There are no special substances, no hidden animating principles. Thought, emotion, identity—each of these can be traced back to neural patterns, electrochemical gradients, and biological evolution. The story it tells is coherent and parsimonious. But coherence is not the same as completeness.

The more that is learned about the brain, the more impressive its mechanisms appear. Yet the question remains: why should any of this be felt? Why should a system that processes information suddenly possess a point of view? The circuitry may be complex, but complexity alone does not imply interiority. The shapes of synapses and the timing of neurotransmitters can be measured in extraordinary detail, but none of this describes what it is like to see red, to remember a song, or to feel sorrow. These are not the behaviors of a system. They are experiences.

This is the persistent challenge to physicalism. The problem is not that the model fails to describe cognition, but that it fails to explain consciousness as such. There is a difference between the function of a system and the presence of a world. A machine may respond to light, but it does not see. It may detect injury, but it does not suffer. Physicalism explains the scaffolding of awareness, but not the fact that anything is aware within it.

Some defenders of this view accept the gap and attempt to dissolve it. They claim that subjective experience is an illusion—a narrative told by the brain to itself. Yet this position is fragile. To call consciousness an illusion is to misunderstand what is being questioned. Illusions, too, are experienced. If the thing being denied still appears, it has not been explained away.

The question is not how the brain produces thought, but why it produces a world. If all physical description is structural and relational, it cannot generate intrinsic qualitative presence from scratch; such presence must already be in the base. This question remains open—not because it is unsophisticated, but because it may point to something physicalism cannot contain. And if that is so, then it is not enough to study the brain. We must reconsider the possibility that awareness is not the last thing to appear, but the first.

Mind as Ground, Not Product

To say that mind might come first is not to claim that the world was dreamed into being by a divine intelligence. It is to consider whether awareness, or something like it, is not the result of the universe, but its underlying condition. Not something added late in the sequence, but something implicit from the beginning—inherent in the appearance of being itself.

This idea is difficult to hold, in part because we are so accustomed to locating mind inside the head. Thought is what brains do. Perception is what nervous systems produce. But these assumptions already rest on a model in which mind is secondary. If, instead, awareness is primary, the frame changes. The question is no longer how physical systems generate consciousness. The question becomes: what kind of reality gives rise to both experience and extension?

This shift does not lead to dualism. It does not posit a realm of mind and a realm of matter, somehow parallel and distinct. Nor does it imply that consciousness is a ghost animating the machinery of the world. What it suggests is more subtle: that what we call the physical may be the exterior of something inward. That extension is how awareness appears when viewed from without.

The term *metaphysical idealism* might be applied to this view, but even that label risks misunderstanding. The point is not to reduce the world to thought. It is to ask whether thought, or the possibility of relation, is more fundamental than objects. Whether coherence arises not from collision, but from intelligibility. Whether the laws of nature reflect not mechanical order, but an interior consistency—a logic that does not originate in matter, but in the conditions that make matter meaningful.

This is not a conclusion, but a reorientation. We are no longer at the edge of the physical, looking inward. We are within the mystery of appearance itself, asking what must be true for anything to appear at all. If awareness is not a byproduct of form, but the ground from which form arises, then the world is not built on particles or forces. It is built on the possibility of being known. Here and throughout, "ground" is meant as soil is to a tree—not something apart from what grows, but the silent condition from which growth draws its life. In this sense, it is an atemporal dependence of physical form on an intrinsic, awareness-like base.

Idealism, Panpsychism, and Beyond

If awareness is not a product of matter, then some other relation must hold between them. Over the centuries, philosophers have proposed different ways of expressing that relation—different metaphysical models for understanding how consciousness and the world might be bound together.

These models do not agree in their details, but they share a basic impulse: to treat mind as something more than an accident.

One of the oldest and most ambitious of these is idealism. In its classical form, idealism holds that reality is not made of matter at all, but of mind. The external world, according to this account, is not a substance independent of consciousness, but a structure within it. Matter appears, but only because mind is already present. This does not mean that the world is imaginary, or that it disappears when unobserved. It means that the framework of appearance—space, time, relation—is inseparable from the possibility of experience. The world is not an object. It is a disclosure.

A different approach is found in panpsychism. Where idealism says that everything is in mind, panpsychism says that mind is in everything. It proposes that all matter possesses some form of interiority—some seed of experience, however faint or rudimentary. An atom is not conscious in the way a person is, but it may have a spark of subjectivity, a primitive responsiveness that later gives rise to full awareness. This perspective denies that consciousness ever "emerges" from non-conscious matter; it was always there, in some form, awaiting more complex expressions.

There are also process-oriented theories, in which reality is not built from things but from events—from relations, unfoldings, and acts of becoming. In this view, both mind and matter are manifestations of deeper movements: expressions of change, interaction, and pattern. What is primary is not the object, but the act; not the thing, but the transformation.

Each of these concepts carries difficulties. Idealism risks solipsism. Panpsychism must answer the "combination problem": how countless micro-experiences combine into a unified subject. Process views must explain what gives order to change. None of these are definitive answers. Yet they reflect a shared recognition: that treating mind as a late-stage phenomenon fails to capture what is most immediate about being. Something is present. Something is aware. Any philosophy that ignores that fact begins in abstraction, not in life.

What Kind of Mind?

If mind is taken as fundamental, care must be taken not to slip into familiar projections. The term itself is saturated with associations—identity, agency, memory, thought. But these are features of human minds, not necessarily of mind as such. To project human psychology onto the foundation of being is to mistake a metaphor for a model. The question is not whether the universe thinks, but whether what we call the universe arises from something inward.

Such a ground need not resemble a person. It need not have goals, preferences, or plans. It need not deliberate or decide. In fact, it may not "do" anything in the usual sense at all. To speak of mind in this context is to point toward the possibility that the world is not exterior all the way down—that being, in its most basic expression, includes not just extension but interiority; not just relation, but awareness.

No single term captures this without distortion. "Mind" is too personal, "consciousness" too cognitive, "spirit" too theological. And yet there is a resistance to the idea that reality is wholly indifferent, without witness, wholly blind. There is a quality to appearance that suggests more than mechanism—not because it is benevolent or beautiful, but because it is present.

That presence may not be directional. It may not guide or watch or intend in any familiar sense. But it may be aware, not as a subject among others, but as the field in which subjects arise. Awareness not as a possession, but as a condition. Not centered, but pervasive. Not bounded, but prior—not a who, but a how.

Such a conception does not suggest that the universe is thinking, or that it has intentions in any familiar sense. Rather, it suggests that what we call mind may be a sign of something deeper: a reality in which awareness is not an outcome, but a background condition; not an event, but a field; not something that happens, but something in which happening becomes possible. In this framing, the presence experienced in human awareness may not be an anomaly, but an echo—a localized flash of something more fundamental. Mind not as explanation, but as openness; not as intellect, but as the capacity for appearance.

The Mirror of the World

If mind is not a product of matter, but something more basic—if it is ground rather than artifact—then the relation to the world must also be reimagined. We are not simply observers of a physical universe, positioned late in the sequence, decoding a logic we did not shape. We are expressions of the same condition that gives rise to everything else. The awareness within us may not be unique. It may be a reflection, a local intensity of something that was present from the beginning.

This is not to say that the world is conscious in the way we are. It is to say that consciousness, in any form, reveals something about what kind of reality is possible. If awareness can appear, then reality cannot be entirely indifferent. If there is subjectivity, there must be more than mechanism. And if something is given—to us, in us, through us—then we are not standing outside the world, but within its unfolding.

The cosmos then is not merely intelligible. It is interior. The laws described by science are not imposed from without but inferred from within. And the act of perception is not passive. It is participatory. To know is not only to observe; it is to co-arise with what is known. In the metaphysical sense introduced in the previous chapter, the same base that could be expressed as non-personal intention there may here be expressed as a mind-like ground. The structure of the world and the structure of awareness may not be parallel by accident. They may be mirrors of the same source.

This does not mean that mind created the world in any simplistic sense. It means that the appearance of the world cannot be fully explained without reference to what allows appearance in the first place. Awareness is not an epilogue to matter. It is the condition under which anything can be said to appear at all.

We do not see the world. We see through it.

CHAPTER 9

The Hiddenness of the Creator

Why the Origin of Being Withholds Its Name

If being was chosen—if the appearance of the world reflects not only possibility, but intention—then a question arises almost immediately: why is that intention not more apparent? If reality was brought forth in freedom, or as a gesture, or from something like will, why does it not bear the marks of that origin? Why does the world look as if it made itself?

Still, the source we are pointing toward—however abstract, however concealed—may be understood by some as divine. We do not name it here, but we do not deny that name. If the source is divine, it is not something that exists within being, nor something that emerged from nothing. It is not part of reality as we know it, or as we can imagine it. It does not exist within any framework. It is what makes being—and even the contrast between being and nothing—possible. When I say "beyond being," I do not mean somewhere else in space or in another realm. I mean that it is not a thing within the contrast it makes possible. Language here is necessarily indirect, using analogy or negation, because there is no direct description available for what lies outside the very categories that make description possible. And in that sense, it is not here. Not hidden, but beyond.

To speak this way is to stretch the limits of understanding. We are not equipped to picture what lies beyond being and nonbeing. Every thought we have is shaped by relation, structure, and time. So we cannot grasp the source. We can only reach toward it—and even that reach may falter. If being was given, it is not unreasonable to imagine a giver—not a being within creation, but the condition for creation itself, outside both something and nothing. And though we resist personifying what remains hidden, we also recognize that what gives rise to presence, silently and without force, has long been called God.

This is the puzzle of concealment. The universe presents itself as lawful, intelligible, and continuous, but not declared. It does not announce its origin. It offers no inscription, no final cause, no unmistakable sign that it was willed. The appearance of matter and mind, order and awareness, may be astonishing, but they do not point unmistakably to a source. They are consistent with emergence. They can be framed as accident. They do not require intention to be described, and they do not confirm it when assumed.

This silence is not new. It is one of the oldest tensions in metaphysical thought: that if there is a source, it remains hidden. The cosmos does not speak of its ground. It does not explain why it exists. It allows for inquiry, but provides no ultimate answer. For many, this has been a cause of despair. If something chose being, then its refusal to be known can feel like abandonment—or worse, indifference.

But there is another possibility. The silence may not be absence. It may be a feature of the kind of world that has been made possible. If the source is not part of the world, it cannot appear within it as one object among others. And if its way of giving is non-coercive—never forcing itself upon what it sustains—then the world it makes will be one in which the evidence for its existence can always be read more than one way. This kind of hiddenness is not a tactic; it is the natural shape of a world made to be free. If intention exists, it may be present in the very structure of that possibility—not as a voice, but as an opening. Not as a command, but as an invitation.

That possibility is what this chapter will explore.

A World Without Signature

If the world was chosen, it does not declare itself. There is no visible mark left behind, no inscription at the origin, no signature at the edge of the stars. The laws of physics describe how things move and interact, but they do not explain why those laws exist, or why there is anything to be governed at all. The structures of reality are remarkably stable—elegant, even—but they do not speak. They allow life, and thought, and wonder, but they do not explain themselves.

This absence of signature leaves us in a strange position. We live in a world shaped by pattern and precision, yet it offers no closure. The very coherence of things invites interpretation—it suggests there should be an answer—but none arrives. The structure of the universe feels intelligible, even meaningful, but it does not declare what that meaning is. This tension can be disorienting. For those who long for revelation, the silence may feel like rejection. For others, it may feel like a freedom—a refusal to collapse meaning into a single message. But for all of us, it presents a challenge: to live within a cosmos that is open to understanding, but not obligated to explain itself.

This silence can be read in many ways. It can be seen as confirmation of indifference—a universe that is simply there, without cause or care. It can also be seen as the absence of coercion, the refusal to dominate, the humility of a ground that does not insist on being known. And because the same quiet could be explained in many ways—including accident or malice—it raises the question: why read it as the sign of a non-coercive giving source rather than as indifference? The answer is not proof but fit: when we look at the whole picture—lawfulness, the reality of interior awareness, the reliable possibility of goods like love, creativity, and truth-seeking— these sit more comfortably with a ground that gives without forcing than with a world that is purely indifferent.

But in either case, the result is the same: we are not given certainty. We are given presence without explanation.

Outside the Frame: God and the Question of Origin

If there is intention behind being, then that intention did not arise within the world. It is not one more process among processes, nor one more mind among minds. It does not act from within the system. It stands outside it—not spatially or temporally, but ontologically. The source of all things cannot be a part of what it gives rise to.

And if being began from absolute nothingness—without structure, contrast, or possibility—then the source must lie not just beyond the world, but beyond all condition. It cannot emerge from logic, potential, or awareness, because none of these existed. When I say it "precedes logic," I do not mean it violates reason. I mean that logic itself belongs to the order of being; the source makes logic possible and is not bound by the categories it gives rise to.

If there is a God, then that God does not emerge from being, nor from nothingness. God is not a product of instability or a byproduct of form. God is not subject to the conditions that structure existence. Even absolute nothingness—the absence of contrast, law, potential, and relation—does not contain or constrain what precedes it. God is not within the frame of explanation. God is what makes explanation possible.

Such a source is not a part of reality—not in space, not in time, not in any realm we can imagine. It is not a being among other beings, nor an alternative to being. It does not exist within the world or outside it, but beyond the entire contrast between presence and absence. It is not something that can be found, because it is what makes finding possible. When I use phrases like "gives rise," I mean them as metaphors for grounding—an atemporal dependence of what is on that which is not itself a thing among things.

Theologies of Hiddenness (and Why They Don't Satisfy)

The hiddenness of the source is not a new concern. Within the traditions of theistic religion, it has long been a subject of meditation, anxiety, and interpretation. Why does God remain silent? Why is the world not filled with obvious signs of divine presence? Why does suffering go unanswered, and faith remain uncertain? These questions are as old as scripture, and they have generated countless attempts at explanation.

Some argue that concealment is necessary for freedom. If the divine were unmistakable, then belief would not be chosen—it would be compelled. Others suggest that hiddenness is a test: of trust, of perseverance, of love unprovoked by proof. Still others propose that the divine is not absent, but hidden only to those unwilling to see. These responses have emotional resonance. They attempt to reconcile the world as it appears with the idea of a personal, relational source. But they do so by attributing reasons to the silence, as if it were strategic—as if the hiddenness were part of a divine psychology.

What they do not address is the possibility that the hiddenness is not a function of personality at all. That it is not chosen in the way a person hides, or designed to produce specific effects. The silence may not be instrumental. It may be structural. It may be what it looks like when being emerges from will without ego—when presence arises not to be recognized, but to be given.

This view does not oppose theology, but it moves beneath it. It asks what kind of metaphysical ground would give rise to a world like this: patterned, coherent, open to inquiry, capable of beauty and cruelty, thought and indifference—and yet without signature. It suggests that the source, if there is one, does not command attention. It allows attention. It makes space for beings who are not forced to know, but free to wonder—and perhaps to choose.

Silence as Condition

If intention remains hidden, it may be because silence is necessary. Not as a strategy, and not as punishment, but as the very condition that makes space for a world like this—open, self-organizing, uncertain, and free. A world in which presence is given, but not declared. In which meaning is possible, but never imposed.

This is not the silence of abandonment. It is the silence of restraint. Of a source that gives without enclosing, that sustains without dictating, that lets its expression unfold without overtaking it. If being arises from will, then it may be a will that withdraws as it gives—a will that makes room rather than occupying it.

We often ask for a sign. But a sign might undo the very thing the world makes possible. In a world made to be free, even those who seek earnestly may find that the available signs are never decisive. They can always be interpreted in more than one way. Beauty, conscience, moral encounter—all of these can be experienced as hints, but none compel agreement.

Perhaps what matters is not whether the source speaks, but whether it holds still long enough for anything else to speak. Perhaps the silence is not waiting to be broken. Perhaps it is what allows everything else to begin.

We tend to think of silence as absence—as the withholding of voice, or the failure to speak. But in a deeper sense, silence can be a form of offering. It makes space. It does not compel. It allows something other than itself to emerge. If the source of being is silent, it may be because it is not trying to direct what follows. It is not waiting to be acknowledged. It is giving without condition. And in doing so, it leaves room for freedom—not just to act, but to interpret, to seek, to believe or not believe, to do good or turn away.

In this light, silence is not a barrier to revelation. It is what makes revelation possible, and what ensures that, if it happens, it will be real.

Intention Without Revelation

If there is intention behind being, it is unlike anything we normally associate with intention. It does not assert itself. It does not make itself known. There is no revelation in the traditional sense—no unveiling of purpose, no message delivered, no will made explicit. What we find instead is a world that is open-ended: coherent, responsive, intelligible—but unclaimed.

This is not what most people imagine when they hear the word "intention." We expect a signal, a direction, a reason. We imagine a mind with goals, a presence with plans. But the kind of intention we are considering here does not behave like that. It does not guide from behind the scenes or write its signature into the laws of nature. It is not hidden in a place we have yet to look. It is hidden in the nature of presence itself.

To give without revealing is not to conceal. It is to allow. A reality that was chosen, but not announced, may be one that refuses to override the freedom of those who live within it. The silence of the source is not the silence of absence, but the refusal to interrupt. It does not disclose itself because it does not demand to be known. If approached in this light, disclosure can only be of a kind that preserves openness: personal or communal, perhaps, but never beyond dispute, never closing the circle.

Such a source, if it exists, cannot be located. It cannot be demonstrated. It can only be inferred from the kind of world we inhabit: one that makes awareness possible, but does not define its meaning. One that gives rise to wonder, but never answers it directly. One that holds back just enough for moral freedom to matter. The source, if there is one, is not something hidden within the world. It is what makes a world possible in the first place—and remains forever beyond it. And to try to comprehend such a source is to bring it back into the world it makes possible—when its very nature is to stand beyond. It may appear paradoxical from within our ordinary ways of thinking. But it is not a contradiction. It is what thought meets when it reaches the edge of its own framework—what arises when the tools we use to understand reality no longer apply. The source does not defy logic; it grounds it. It is not something we can grasp from within the system it makes possible.

Living in the Absence

To live in a world that may have been chosen, but does not reveal its chooser, is to live in ambiguity. We are surrounded by structure, by beauty, by intelligibility. We are also surrounded by suffering, by randomness, by silence. The temptation is always to resolve the tension—either by declaring that there is no intention, or by assigning that intention a name, a purpose, a voice. But perhaps the tension is the point.

The absence of revelation is not the absence of meaning. It is the refusal to make meaning automatic. A world with hidden origins is not necessarily a world without ground. It may be one in which the ground remains still—allowing what arises to unfold on its own terms. In such a world, meaning is not imposed. It is made possible.

And with it, so is responsibility. For in a world that does not declare itself, we are free to answer or ignore, to care or dismiss, to align ourselves with what feels good, or what is good. To live with such freedom is not to be abandoned. It is to be entrusted.

Some may see in this silence not the absence of God, but the way divinity gives without imposition. If the source remains unnamed, it may be because it does not demand recognition. It entrusts the world to itself. And for those who do hear something in that silence—however faint—it may not be a message, but an offering: presence without pressure, meaning without command, love without signature.

This requires a different kind of attention. Not belief, and not skepticism, but attunement. A readiness to live without resolution. A willingness to let the silence remain. To treat the lack of disclosure not as a void to be filled, but as an opening to be received.

We do not need the source to speak in order to respond.

But we may be here, in part, to choose how.

CHAPTER 10

When Meaning Must Be Chosen

Freedom, Silence, and the Ethics of Response

I f there is intention at the origin of being, it is not the kind that speaks. It does not declare its purpose, explain its design, or command recognition. It allows a world to appear, but it does not interpret that world on our behalf. There is no statement of meaning, no moral direction etched into the fabric of space. And yet, the possibility of intention persists—not as doctrine, but as hypothesis. Not in what the world says, but in that it is here to be spoken with. If such intention exists, it does not emerge from being or dwell within it. It stands beyond the world it makes possible—ungraspable, but not unreachable.

And if it stands beyond the world, it does so not as something distant in space or time, but as something wholly other. It does not arise from possibility or operate within conditions. It gives rise to condition itself. If it exists, it cannot be part of any structure we can conceive—not even potential, not even logic. Here "beyond logic" does not mean a license for contradiction. It means that logic itself belongs to the world the source makes possible; the source is what gives logic its footing. It is not hidden in the world. It is what makes a world, and meaning, possible at all.

When I speak of "meaning" in this chapter, I do not mean a single, monolithic thing. There is *cosmic meaning*—any ultimate purpose or goal for reality as a whole. There is *moral meaning*—our stance toward good and evil and the reasons for acting as we do. And there is *personal meaning*—the felt significance of our lives. Here, the concern is with moral and personal meaning in a world where cosmic meaning, if it exists, remains silent.

This raises a sharper version of the question we've been approaching throughout this part of the book: Can meaning arise without being imposed? If being was chosen, does that imply a purpose? And if so, why does that purpose remain silent? These questions are not only metaphysical. They are existential. They ask what kind of life is possible in a world where meaning is never guaranteed.

The temptation is to frame the absence as failure. If the source is silent, then perhaps there is no source. If the universe is undirected, then perhaps it is empty. But that logic assumes that intention must behave like authority—that if being was chosen, it must also have been directed, shaped, defined. Yet the deepest possibilities of intention may lie not in determination, but in restraint. In the refusal to compel. In the creation of a space where meaning does not descend from above, but rises from within.

This chapter begins from that possibility: that the universe may be an act of freedom whose deepest offering is the freedom it extends to others. That if being was chosen, it was not chosen to fulfill a plan—but to allow the unfolding of lives capable of finding meaning, or not, on their own terms.

Freedom Without Abandonment

In a universe governed by silence, it is easy to feel alone. The absence of instruction, the lack of disclosure, the refusal to make meaning obvious—these can feel like abandonment. If we are here without a message, without a revealed purpose, then perhaps there is no meaning to find. But this conclusion assumes that freedom and care cannot coexist. That silence is always a sign of indifference.

There is another way to read the silence. It may be the condition under which meaning becomes possible. In a world where the source does not speak, nothing is predetermined. Meaning is not prescribed, so it must be discovered. If being was chosen, then perhaps it was not chosen to enact a design, but to open a space in which something unforced could arise. Something that is not the fulfillment of a will, but the response to a gift.

Such a view requires a different understanding of intention. Not as authorship, but as offering. Not as a voice that speaks into the world, but as the condition that allows a world to speak at all. This is not the intention of control, but the intention of invitation—an invitation understood here as an analogy for the effects of a non-coercive ground, not a literal expression of will. The presence of structure without imposition. The presence of possibility without certainty.

To be free in this sense is not to be abandoned. It is to be trusted. Trusted to become, to ask, to err, to choose. Freedom here need not depend on indeterminism; it is enough that we are not compelled, and that we can respond to reasons, however we come by them. The silence of the source is not the silence of emptiness. It is the silence of restraint. It is what allows our questions to be real, our meanings to matter, our lives to unfold without coercion.

A World That Waits for Us to Choose

If the source is silent, it may be because we are meant to respond. Not with certainty, but with freedom. If there is a God who chose to give rise to a world, then perhaps that world was not created to showcase power or declare a plan. Perhaps it was given as a space of possibility—a world not of answers, but of choices.

To believe or not.

To love or not.

To do good or evil.

This may be the most serious feature of our condition: that we are not only free to live, but free to decide what kind of beings we will become. That in a universe where nothing is compelled, even goodness must be chosen. Even belief must be offered freely.

This view does not trivialize morality. It deepens it. For in a world without imposed direction, good and evil are not "just" social constructions or evolutionary conveniences. They are existential orientations—ways of standing in relation to others and to reality. Whether we ground these in minimal objective facts about conscious life (for example, that gratuitous harm is wrong) or in the fitting responses of well-functioning agents, they remain more than preference. One orientation leans toward generosity, care, and attention. The other toward domination, indifference, or harm. The difference between them is not always obvious—but it is real.

And it matters that we are free to choose between them. A world that allows evil is not one that endorses it. It is one that permits freedom—and with it, the risk and weight of what we do. That freedom, terrible and beautiful, may not be an accident. It may be the very reason we are here.

Meaning Without Guarantees

A world that does not declare its meaning is a world that allows meaning to be real. If meaning is not embedded in the structure of things—if it is not given in advance—then whatever meaning we find must be discovered, created, or received through relation. It cannot be assumed. It cannot be extracted as fact. And it cannot be forced.

This kind of world demands more from us than one in which purpose is clear. In the absence of revelation, we are left to make sense of things without assurance. The beauty we find is not assigned. The suffering we face is not explained. The choices we make are not confirmed by an external source. There is no blueprint, no voice to tell us we are right. And yet, meaning still arises—in art, in care, in memory, in love.

But these meanings are fragile. They do not hold the weight of proof. They cannot be imposed on others. They cannot even be fully secured within ourselves. They are not structures. They are responses—always provisional, always personal, always incomplete. The price of freedom is that meaning is never guaranteed.

That is also what makes it real. Meaning that is not assigned must be lived. It arises in how we respond—not once, but again and again—in care, in attention, in the risks we take to affirm what cannot be proven. This is why the silence of the source can be seen as a gift: certain goods—love, courage, fidelity, honest inquiry—depend on being chosen freely. If the source declared itself with unmistakable force, these goods could be replaced by compliance. We are not given a script. We are given a field of possibility, and the freedom to shape it. A silent gift still calls for an answer. It does not instruct us, but it waits.

Love, Attention, and the Refusal to Compel

If the source of being is silent, it may not be because it is absent, but because it refuses to compel. This is not a silence born of distance, but of a deeper kind of generosity—the kind that gives without controlling, that invites without demanding, that holds space for freedom rather than filling it. Such a gesture, if it exists, bears a resemblance to what we call love—again, not literally, but as an analogy to describe the effect of non-coercion.

Love, at its most authentic, does not seek to override. It does not impose itself, or guarantee reciprocation, or inscribe its meaning in advance. It waits. It attends. It allows the other to appear as they are, not as they are required to be. If the universe was chosen into being, then perhaps it was chosen in something like this spirit—not as a project to be fulfilled, but as a space in which relationship becomes possible.

In this light, attention becomes an ethical act. Not the attention of analysis or control, but of presence. To attend is to make room. To witness without grasping. To live without reducing. If the world is silent, it may be because it is listening. And if it was willed, then perhaps that will was not to be known, but to be met.

Meaning, in such a world, does not arrive prefigured. It emerges through attention. It takes shape in the way we respond—to each other, to the world, to the silence. The refusal to compel is not a withholding of meaning. It is what makes meaning matter.

The Universe as an Invitation

We have imagined many things about the universe—that it is random, that it is law-bound, that it is indifferent, that it is meaningful. But perhaps what we are seeing is not a declaration or a design. Perhaps it is an invitation. The presence of intelligibility, the capacity for awareness, the freedom to respond—all of these may point not to an argument, but to a possibility. Not to a conclusion, but to a relationship that has not yet been defined.

An invitation does not arrive with force. It does not explain itself. It does not command assent. It offers itself, and waits. The world may be like this—open, coherent, responsive, but withholding its meaning until meaning is made. If being was chosen, perhaps it was not chosen for a purpose to be fulfilled, but for a freedom to be lived. A world given, not to satisfy a plan, but to become something more through what it allows.

This does not lessen the mystery. It deepens it. It asks us to live without guarantees, but not without hope. To live as if something has been offered—not proved, not demanded, not secured—but offered nonetheless. Not a message to be decoded, but a presence to be answered.

Meaning as Response, Not Proof

If the universe does not assert its meaning, then whatever meaning it holds must emerge in response. Not as certainty, but as relation. Not as deduction, but as participation. We are not offered an answer. We are given a world. And that world, in its silence and openness, becomes the ground on which our lives unfold.

In such a universe, meaning is not something we uncover like a buried structure. It is something we shape, slowly and incompletely, through how we meet what is. Through how we live, how we behold, how we care. The absence of guarantees is not a flaw in the design. It is what allows any meaning to be genuine.

It is also why the same freedom that allows authentic meaning also allows harm—echoing the account in Chapter 9, where the universe's silence was described as a non-coercive opening rather than a demand. If reality leans toward presence, it does so without forcing recognition.

This is the final gesture of a non-coercive universe: that we are not told what the world is for, but asked what we will do with it. That we are not given answers, but given time. That we are not shown the source, but allowed to wonder if one is there.

In the silence, something has been offered. What we make of it is our reply.

PART IV
Being, Time, and US

When the Question Becomes a Life

We began with the question of why anything exists. But the deeper question may be how to live in the presence of what does.

We have followed the question of existence from the silence of nothing to the possibility of intention. We have considered whether the world was born from law or from will, whether its coherence reflects structure or expression, whether consciousness is an accident or a mirror. Each chapter has pressed against the limit of explanation—not to escape mystery, but to recognize it.

But now the question returns in a different form. It is no longer abstract. It is personal. If something like intention gave rise to being, then we are not observing a world—we are living within it. And if freedom was part of that gift, then how we live becomes part of the unfolding. Our bodies, our time, our choices, our losses—all take place in this same offering. Whatever the origin, we are among its consequences. And the question is no longer only why is there something rather than nothing?—but what are we to do with the something we are given?

This final part turns to the human dimension—not as a retreat from metaphysics, but as its natural continuation. If the source does not compel belief, and if goodness must be chosen, then our freedom is not incidental. It is part of the structure. If the universe does not declare meaning but makes it possible, then how we respond becomes central. In these final chapters, we reflect on what it means to be temporal, mortal, conscious, and capable of love in a world that remains silent. Not to solve the question, but to learn how to live in its light—and in its shadow.

CHAPTER 11

Living in the Wake of the Question

How We Respond to a World That Won't Explain Itself

T he question of existence does not go away. Even when we are not thinking of it, it lingers beneath our lives—the silent tension between appearance and origin, between what is and what might never have been. We go about our days in the company of this mystery, often unaware of its presence, until some moment breaks the surface: a death, a birth, a silence too wide to ignore. Then the riddle returns. And not as theory, but as atmosphere.

We do not live outside this question. We live within it. Not as philosophers, but as persons. Our lives unfold in a world that remains unexplained, but not indifferent. A world that is coherent but unsigned. We eat, speak, mourn, remember, and hope inside a reality that does not declare itself. We live in the wake of a question that may never be answered—and yet it shapes everything we do.

The silence we explored in earlier chapters is not just metaphysical. It is lived. It is the silence in which we make meaning, the absence in which we offer love, the uncertainty under which we make choices. We are not given clarity, but we are given time. And time is not neutral. It moves us forward while leaving nothing behind. In the absence of revelation, it is time that asks how we will live.

And if time asks how we will live, the deeper question asks why there is life to live at all.

We have already wondered whether the fact of our existence might be the result of intention—not a plan unfolding in time, but a giving that stands wholly outside both something and nothing, beyond every category being contains. If so, intention would not be a thing among things, nor a ghost within the void, but the threshold itself: the place where absence gives way to presence without compulsion. Seen in this light, our being here is not an accident, nor a necessity, but a gift without claim—a freedom that asks how we will live within it.

To be human is not to solve the mystery, but to remain faithful to what is entrusted.

Such fidelity may not explain our existence, but it allows us to live as though our being were a gift, and our lives a reply.

The Weight of Consciousness

To be aware is to be exposed. We do not simply exist—we know that we exist. We remember what has passed and anticipate what is coming. We reflect on our thoughts, imagine what others feel, wonder what it all means. This capacity is extraordinary. It allows for art, for love, for grief, for loyalty, for longing. It makes possible everything we think of as human. But it also carries a weight nothing else seems to bear.

Consciousness reveals the fragility of things. It allows us to see beauty—but also to see that beauty fades. It allows us to remember joy—but also to remember what we have lost. It is through consciousness that we love, and through consciousness that we grieve. The same awareness that opens the world to us also opens us to sorrow, regret, and the knowledge of death.

We sometimes treat this burden as a problem to be solved. We numb it, distract from it, theorize it away. But the weight is not an error. It may be the deepest truth of our condition: that we are alive in a world that will not last, and that we know this. We are here—we are aware that we are here, and nothing in our experience remains untouched by time.

We are not wounded by consciousness. Consciousness makes us.

Time as Exposure

We do not pass through time. We are changed by it. Every experience we have is marked by before and after. Every joy is framed by its eventual ending. Every loss is shaped by its irreversibility. Time does not just move us forward—it opens us to the reality that things change, decay, disappear. And in that exposure, we come to know what matters.

To be in time is to be unable to return. It is to remember what can never be relived, to anticipate what cannot be controlled, to live through moments that cannot be secured. This irreversibility is not an abstraction. It is felt. It is the way a goodbye echoes, the way a child grows, the way a loved one becomes memory.

It is this very exposure that allows for meaning. Without time, there would be no urgency, no stakes, no beauty in the passing. The finitude of life does not negate its value—it makes value possible. A world without endings would be a world without significance, a world in which nothing was ever at risk.

Time does not steal meaning. It reveals it. We do not recognize what matters because it lasts. We recognize it because it doesn't.

The Human Response: Making, Remembering, Attending

In the absence of certainty, we act. Not always with clarity, and not always with success, but with an impulse to respond to the world rather than endure it. When the question of meaning is not resolved from beyond us, we seek it from within—not with answers, but with responses. Through creating significance, remembering, and staying present, we begin to live as if meaning were still possible, even if never secured.

We make. We shape sound, image, movement, and symbol. We compose poems and prayers, songs and stories—not to declare truth, but to keep what feels necessary. Art becomes a way of living in mystery without explanation. It does not resolve the silence, but it allows us to speak into it. In this sense, making is not a claim but a participation—a way of meeting the world that does not pretend to understand it, yet refuses to remain passive before it.

We remember. Not only the facts of what has occurred, but the weight of what has mattered. Memory is not recollection. It is a form of honoring—a way of preserving what time threatens to erase. In remembering, we refuse the idea that only the present is real. We allow what is no longer here to continue shaping what we are. The act of remembering is a silent defiance against disappearance.

And we keep watch. We pay attention to what is fragile, fleeting, unresolved. We learn to stay with what we do not control. To remain present is to live without mastery, to let the world disclose itself on its own terms. It is not passivity. It is the discipline of receptivity—the practice of being present without needing to possess. Attention is perhaps the most difficult of these responses, and the most important. For in a world that does not declare its meaning, what we carry in awareness becomes what we hold sacred.

These responses do not solve the mystery. They do not eliminate pain or answer the question. But they orient us. They make it possible to live inside uncertainty without collapsing into despair or nihilism. To make, to remember, to attend—these are not strategies of resolution. They are acts of relationship. They are how we live in the shadow of the question.

And in the end, to make, to remember, and to attend—these become not ways of surviving the unknown, but ways of caring for what we do not fully understand. In their quiet insistence, such acts say: this matters, even if we cannot say why.

Not Resolution, but Return

We are often taught to seek closure, to resolve uncertainty, to find meaning in a final form. But the deepest questions do not close. They remain open not because they are flawed, but because they are fundamental. They are not puzzles to be solved, but conditions we live within. The question of being—why anything exists, why we are aware, why the world is as it is—does not disappear in the presence of science, philosophy, or faith. It endures.

And it endures not only in thought, but in experience. We feel it in time, in loss, in love. We feel it in moments of beauty we cannot explain, in grief we cannot contain, in the weight of decisions we must make without knowing what they mean. The question is not abstract. It moves through us. It becomes us.

To live in the wake of the question is not to wait for an answer. It is to return to it, again and again, not with despair, but with fidelity. To live as if meaning might still be made. To live as if presence matters, even if its origin remains hidden. This is not a solution. It is a way of remaining in relation. Not resolution. It is return—a repeated, faithful turning back toward the question.

CHAPTER 12

When Time Becomes Mortal

How Death Defines What Matters

We often imagine death as something that happens to us, as an event that arrives at the end of life to take it away. It feels like an interruption—a break in the flow of time, a tearing away from everything known and loved. But death is not separate from life. It is not an intrusion. It is part of the very essence that makes life what it is.

Without death, there would be no urgency. No moment would matter more than another. Nothing would need to be chosen now. Everything could be deferred. The weight of decision would dissolve. Relationships would stretch on without risk. Grief would lose its shape. Love would lose its depth. Mortality is what gives our moments form and contour. It presses time into meaning.

To be mortal is not only to die. It is to live in the knowledge that life cannot be held. That what is given will be taken. That everything we touch, everything we love, will one day slip beyond our grasp. This is not a flaw in the design. It is the condition for any design to matter. Death gives shape to attention. It is the limit that reveals what lies within.

We do not live toward death as toward a wall. We live through it as a frame. It is not what stands at the end of meaning, but what stands around it—clarifying it, intensifying it, making it real.

The Illusion of Escape

We live in a time that rarely speaks of death directly. It is softened, postponed, managed. It is hidden behind medical language, obscured by euphemism, displaced by entertainment. When it must be named, it is often treated as a failure—a lapse in progress, a defect in design, a challenge to be overcome. Beneath this impulse lies an ancient hope: that death can be escaped, or at least deferred long enough to become irrelevant.

Sometimes this hope takes the form of distraction. We fill our days with noise and novelty, as if to stay just ahead of the awareness that everything we love will pass. At other times it becomes ambition—a drive to leave a mark, to be remembered, to extend the arc of life through achievement or legacy. More recently, it has taken technological form: visions of radical life extension, digital preservation, or the engineering of human immortality. In each case, the promise is the same: to slip the constraint of finitude.

Literature has long imagined such an escape. In Oscar Wilde's *The Picture of Dorian Gray*, the portrait carries the burden of time while its subject remains untouched. Yet what first appears like freedom corrodes into emptiness. Released from the press of mortality, Dorian's life does not deepen but unravels, beauty withering into decay and intimacy into emptiness.

But the pursuit of escape risks erasing the very structure that gives life its weight. Death is not an error to be fixed. It is the horizon that makes experience precious. A life without end may feel like freedom, but it dissolves the texture of time. Without loss, there is no urgency. Without urgency, there is no meaning. We do not need to welcome death—but to treat it only as a flaw is to forget what it discloses.

To live well is not to defeat mortality. It is to learn how to live in the presence of it, with full knowledge that the thread will be cut. Escape may seem like a solution, but it is a refusal of the very condition that allows anything to matter. To refuse death is to refuse the frame. But to live within it, knowingly, is to engage the world with presence. Not to escape its finitude, but to inhabit it more fully.

Longevity as Reverence, Not Rebellion

To live longer is not inherently to reject mortality. It can be an act of reverence. The desire to extend life need not come from fear or denial. It can come from attention—a recognition that life is not just bearable but beautiful, not just accidental but meaningful. It can arise not from a refusal to die, but from a deepened desire to remain in relation to what is.

In this light, longevity becomes something more than survival. It becomes a form of gratitude. To preserve the body is not to cling to it at all costs, but to care for the time it holds. The body is not a prison to be escaped, but a vessel through which attention moves. A longer life, if lived wisely, may not diminish mortality's meaning, but may widen it. It may offer more time to love, to learn, to remember, to make.

There is a danger, of course, in turning longevity into conquest—treating time as a resource to be hoarded, or death as a defect to be engineered away. But when longevity is pursued with humility, it can become a form of fidelity. Not a rebellion against death, but a way of honoring the life that death frames.

Not a rejection of endings, but a deepening of presence.

The Time That Remains

Time is not what we manage. It is what we are given. We do not own it, measure it, or save it—not in any ultimate sense. It flows through us and around us, carrying everything we are and everything we will lose. And yet, in that passing, it also gives. It gives form to presence, depth to memory, and shape to becoming. The time that remains is not the time we control, but the time we respond to.

To live in time is to live within rhythms—some chosen, some imposed, some barely perceptible until they shift. We age, we forget, we anticipate, we repeat. In these movements, time becomes a medium of relation. It is how we hold what has passed, how we reach toward what is to come, and how we remain with what is now. Time is not neutral. It marks us. It invites us. It asks what we will do with what remains.

There is no answer to that question that fits all lives. Some spend their time in urgency, others in stillness. Some in care, others in retreat. But beneath every form of life is the same condition: time that cannot be returned, only received. To live well is not to master that time. It is to meet it, moment by moment, with whatever honesty and attention we can bring. In the face of uncertainty, that meeting may be the most meaningful thing we ever do.

Death and the Question It Keeps Alive

There is no escaping the fact of death. It is written into the tissue of what we are—biologically, temporally, existentially. We will leave, and so will everyone we love. We know this, and yet we go on living as if what we do matters. We love knowing we will grieve. We create knowing it will pass. We act as if meaning can outlast the body that holds it.

This tension has haunted human consciousness from the beginning. Some treat it as evidence of delusion—a desperate attempt to resist the obvious. Others treat it as evidence of something more: a longing that might not be explained by evolutionary pressure or cultural habit. A longing for significance that does not vanish, for presence that does not collapse into absence, for a response that is not absorbed into silence. We do not know whether that longing points beyond us. But we feel it. And we shape our lives around it.

Even if that longing has no object, it reveals something essential about us. It shows that we are not content with the visible, not satisfied with the temporary. We are creatures who reach—toward permanence, toward understanding, toward love that does not end. Whether or not anything meets that reach, the reaching itself is real. And it shapes everything we do.

We return, again, to the central question. Not as theory, but as ache. Not as puzzle, but as posture.

And perhaps that is what gives life its meaning—that the question remains, and we are the ones left to answer it.

Death does not silence the question. It intensifies it.

CHAPTER 13

Love, Memory, and the Echo of Intention

How Love Endures When Nothing Is Certain

We love even though we know it will end. This is one of the most ordinary and astonishing truths of human life. We do not wait for guarantees, for permanence, or for clarity. We do not stop to calculate whether it is rational to form bonds that will be broken. We simply love. Parents love children who will leave them. Friends love through illness. Lovers hold each other in the shadow of time. We give ourselves to people, places, and moments we know we cannot keep.

Love is not delayed by mortality. It rises in the face of it. It does not ask whether the one we love will remain, only whether they are here. It does not seek preservation—it seeks presence. This persistence defies explanation. It is not utilitarian. It is not reducible to advantage or survival. It is something else—something that appears again and again in the shape of our lives, even when we know what it will cost.

We learn, over time, that love is not a shelter from loss. It is a form of agreement with it. To love is to say: this matters, even though it will end. Even though it may hurt. Even though it cannot be held. Love does not erase finitude. It intensifies it. It marks what is transient as sacred, and it does so not in denial—but in full awareness of what will pass.

This is not a flaw in our reasoning. It may be a glimpse into what being makes possible. We love not despite our condition, but within it. And perhaps, most profoundly, we love because of it.

Memory as Continuity of the Lost

We remember what is no longer here, and yet somehow remains. A voice, a scent, a glance, a rhythm in how someone spoke or moved—these things persist long after the body has gone. Memory is not a replication. It is not the storing of information. It is the continuation of relationship in another form. It lets us remain connected with what has passed, not by holding it unchanged, but by letting it live again in the space of our attention.

To remember someone is not to think about them. It is to affirm that what they were matters now. It is to carry forward their presence, not as fact but as meaning. In memory, we do not preserve the dead—we stay with them. We let them shape what we see, how we act, what we carry forward. And in doing so, we refuse the idea that time can erase what once was real.

There is something strangely ethical in this. To remember is to give witness. It is to resist the vanishing that time demands. It is to hold open a space where the past is not buried, but honored. In this way, memory becomes more than a feature of consciousness. It becomes a form of care. A way of saying: you are not here, but you are not nothing.

This is not only about others. We remember versions of ourselves—decisions, regrets, acts of love or failure—and these memories are not inert. They continue to shape what we are. We live not in spite of what we remember, but because of it. Memory is not just the trace of being. It is a way being continues.

Love Beyond Survival

Some forms of love do not make sense in evolutionary terms. They do not increase our chances of survival, or extend our genetic line, or secure our comfort. We sit by the bedsides of the dying. We remain faithful to those who cannot return our care. We grieve decades after the person is gone.

We risk ourselves for strangers. We carry the weight of someone else's memory long after it ceases to serve any function at all.

This kind of love resists explanation. It does not ask whether the beloved will change, or whether the love will be returned, or whether anything will come of it. It simply persists. It endures through loss, failure, and silence. Sometimes it even deepens there. It moves not toward advantage, but toward fidelity. Not toward control, but toward presence. In these moments, love seems to forget itself as a strategy. It becomes a form of attention—an unguarded openness to what is.

There is something excessive in this, something that survival alone cannot explain. Yet it is precisely in such acts—humble, costly, often hidden—that we glimpse what is most deeply human. They reveal love as more than instinct, more than preference, more than mutual exchange. Here, love becomes gift: offered without demand, without assurance, without end.

In giving without return, love becomes not only human but possibly reflective—something that resembles the shape of a world given freely, not to command, but to be answered.

This is not evidence of anything beyond us. But it may be a mark. A way of pointing toward the possibility that love is not only something we do, but something we reflect. That in its most self-giving form, love may echo something deeper in the structure of being—something not imposed, but expressed.

The Echo of Intention

If love can move beyond advantage, beyond reciprocation, beyond self-interest, then it may carry something more than emotional weight. It may carry philosophical significance. The question is not whether love demonstrates anything metaphysical—it does not. But it may suggest something. It may hint. It may echo. Not in what it says, but in what it is.

In the earlier chapters we asked whether being could have emerged from intention—not from mechanism, not from necessity, but from something like will; not the will to dominate, but the will to give. If such an origin is even possible, we might ask: what would it look like if intention left a mark, not in law or inscription, but in expression? In sign? In connection?

It would not look like certainty. It would not arrive with force. It would be quiet. It would allow space rather than fill it. It would resemble the kind of love that gives without holding, that offers without requiring, that persists without needing reward. Such love does not declare its source. It simply moves in the world, leaving traces that feel less like evidence and more like invitation.

Not a proof, but a resemblance.

Fidelity to the Invisible

We do not love because we understand. We love because something in us remains open—even in the absence of proof, even when meaning is uncertain, even when loss is inevitable. To love is to remain open to what we cannot possess. It is to give ourselves to what will pass, and still call it real. It is to stand with what disappears and say, this mattered.

This is not an act of belief in the usual sense. It is not a statement about what is true. It is a stance—a way of being-with. A form of fidelity that holds even when nothing holds it in return. We remain faithful not because we know, but because we choose to. Because something in us recognizes that attention, memory, care—these are not reducible to function. They are acts of meaning that live in the space beyond necessity.

In this way, love becomes more than a feeling. It becomes a way of staying near the mystery. A way of responding to a presence that does not explain itself. Not because we are sure of what it means, but because we are willing to abide with it. Not because we possess it, but because we are willing to live as if something has been offered—and to shape our lives as a reply.

CHAPTER 14

Living in the Light of Mystery

The Grace of Not Knowing

We do not arrive at the end of this inquiry with answers. The question with which we began—why there is something rather than nothing—remains. No theory has closed it, no framework contained it. At the far edge of all explanation, the enigma endures. It does not demand belief, nor yield to certainty. It simply continues.

But though the question persists, we are not where we started. We have walked to the boundary of what logic can settle, the fragility of structure, the possibility of intention, and the silence of a world that does not declare its source. We have stood within time, mortality, and love—not as concepts, but as conditions. Through it all, the unknown has changed shape. It is no longer an obstacle to be overcome, but a reality to live with.

This is not closure. It is not a resolution. It is a turning—away from the need to master the question, and toward the possibility of living in relation to it. The riddle has not lessened. But our way of meeting it has taken root in us.

Mystery as Atmosphere

More often, it surrounds us quietly, shaping what we see without naming itself. It is not a boundary we meet at the edge of knowledge. It is the air around all knowing—the background hum of being that never explains itself, but never leaves. It can be sensed in the first light spilling into a hospital corridor after a long night, when nothing is resolved but everything is here, or in the turn toward home after a long absence, when the familiar carries an unexpected weight of strangeness.

We feel it in moments of clarity, and in moments of loss. In the stillness after music ends. In the gaze of someone we love. In the sudden recognition that everything passes. These are not proofs of anything.

They are atmospheres—felt more than understood, closer than described. Something within them resists being reduced to explanation. They do not tell us what the world means. They ask how we are responding to it.

To live with this is not to live in confusion. It is to live with attentiveness—not for what is hidden, but for what is present and unspeakable. Reverence is not about understanding less. It is about recognizing that not everything we grasp must be named. Some realities are not resolved by analysis. They are illuminated by fidelity.

Mystery, in this sense, is not what we encounter only when knowledge fails. It is what sustains us all along.

Attention as Response

If the mystery cannot be solved, it can still be met. One of the most powerful ways we meet it is through attention. To attend is not to analyze or control. It is not passive observation, but participatory relation. It is to make space within ourselves for what is—not to possess it, but to receive it. Attention is active restraint, a discipline of lingering with what we do not fully understand, like lowering our voices at a graveside—not to fill the air with answers, but to keep company with what matters. Such attention becomes a way of standing still before the infinite, as one might pause before a vast horizon.

In a world that does not declare its meaning, attention becomes a form of devotion. It is how we are present to the real, even when the real offers no explanation. This is how we dwell with ambiguity without collapsing into cynicism or denial. Such regard becomes a kind of devotion—a way of saying: I do not know what this means, but I will keep faith with it.

This is not easy. Distraction is simpler; abstraction is safer. But attention, especially toward what is fragile, fleeting, or unresolved, helps us stay human before what we do not understand. It helps us be true to a world that changes us as we move through it. It honors the mystery without trying to master it. In this way, attention becomes a response—not to the question itself, but to the fact that we are here to ask it.

Living Without Knowing

We are not asked to understand everything. We are not required to arrive at certainty in order to live meaningfully. Much of what matters most— love, death, memory, hope—takes place in the absence of final answers. We do not know what follows death. We do not know what the universe is for, or if it is for anything. Still, we go on.

We love, we mourn, we create, we care. We pack up houses after a parent dies, sealing boxes we know we will open years later, carrying questions alongside keepsakes. These acts are not less real because they are performed without guarantees. They may be more real because of it.

To live without certainty is not to live in confusion. It is to live in humility. To recognize that reality does not owe us definition. That truth may not be something we possess, but something we serve. Humility is not a retreat from seriousness; it is a deepening of it. It allows us to live with the open question—not impatiently, not fearfully, but faithfully.

The refusal to force a conclusion is not indifference. It is awe. It is what allows space for the mystery to be what it is—quiet, unresolved, and still worthy of regard. In this way, unknowing becomes a form of wisdom. Not as a destination, but as a way of walking. A way of being open to what the world might still be saying.

And in that openness, something begins to shift. We are no longer waiting for the universe to explain itself. We are waiting to see who we will become in relation to it.

Echoes and Hints

There are moments when the world feels unusually near. Not explained, but illuminated. A line of music, a scent from childhood, the sudden presence of someone we've lost. The faint smell of rain on warm pavement that carries us back to a street we thought we'd forgotten. These are not revelations. They do not untangle the riddle.

But they soften us toward it. They make us pause. They make us wonder if what we call absence is sometimes another form of closeness. These moments are fragile.

They do not last. They resist interpretation. Still, we return to them—not because they answered the question, but because they kept it alive in a different way. They shifted our posture—not toward certainty, but toward awe. They did not resolve the unknown; they made it feel, if only for a moment, like something we could live with.

We should not demand too much from these moments. They are not messages. They are not evidence. They are more like glimmers—traces that move through us and ask for nothing except heed. To live in the light of the unexplained is not to chase these echoes, but to allow them. Not to explain them, but to receive them.

They disclose no final truth. But they change how we dwell in its company.

Light, Not Clarity

We began with the question of why anything exists. We asked whether being could emerge from nothing, whether structure could arise without law, and whether intention—wholly outside both something and nothing—could be present without command. We followed the silence of the world not to escape it, but to listen more carefully to what it allows. And in the end, there was no source we could name. What remained was ground—the place from which life unfolds.

Whether the path that brought us here is read as emergence without law, or as intention with or without a who; whether one imagines awareness as ground, or simply receives the world's coherence as given—the posture it calls for is the same. Attentiveness, humility, and stewardship. The same response, whatever the route.

That ground does not reveal itself. It does not explain its purpose or sign its name. But it gives rise to love, to memory, to time, to longing. It allows for heedfulness and makes room for relation. It offers a world that asks for nothing and still allows us to shape meaning, to grieve well, to respond. It gives us the chance to become who we are, even as we change.

And that nearness may be enough. It may be the quietest form of grace—in the ordinary sense, an unearned openness—a world that holds open the possibility of goodness without insisting on it. A world in which we are free not only to act, but to choose whether to believe, to care, to give. A world that conceals its origin not to withhold, but to entrust.

This is not lucidity. It is not proof or conclusion. But it is something rather than nothing. It is the light that makes it possible to live without resolution. It is what lets us stay close to what we cannot understand, without turning away.

We do not know why there is anything at all. We know only that there is, and that we may answer it—to attend, to to be mindful, to keep faith.

In the absence of answers, we are given the chance to endure. And in that endurance, we may become the kind of beings this mystery was waiting for.

And in the end, that may be enough.

Epilogue

There is no more fundamental question than why anything exists at all. Every other question—about matter, mind, morality, time, love—presumes that something is already here. This one does not.

It asks before there is a before. It pushes past the edge of explanation. And for most of history, it has been deferred, spiritualized, reframed, or ignored. Too large, too strange, too unsettling to hold for long.

But the question remains. It waits—not in the margins of thought, but at its origin.

This book has tried to stay with it. Not to resolve it, but to see how far it can be followed without collapsing into myth or abstraction. Whether being could arise from nothing. Whether structure could emerge without law. Whether intention could give rise to presence without declaring itself. Whether love, grief, memory, and choice are just side effects—or something closer to a reply.

None of this has produced an answer. But it has reshaped the question.

It no longer belongs to philosophy alone. It belongs to anyone who wonders why the world is here—and what it means to live in a world that does not explain itself. Anyone who has sensed that silence does not always mean absence. That mystery is not the same as confusion. That freedom might be part of the structure of things. That the deepest questions are not always meant to be solved, but carried.

If there is a source—of being, of time, of consciousness—it has not announced itself. It has not left instructions. It has given no clear sign that it wishes to be found. What we have is a world. Coherent. Incomplete. Capable of meaning, but unwilling to impose it.

Which leaves the question not only unanswered, but entrusted to us.

There may be other theories, other metaphysical sketches. But nearly all of them reduce, in the end, to some version of the same two paths: either being emerged on its own, or it was given. Either it arose from nothing without cause, or it was willed by something not subject to the conditions it created. All other answers tend to defer the question, redefine it, or dissolve it into formalisms. But the question remains. And when pressed to its foundation, it seems to leave us with just these two possibilities: that we are here because nothing could not hold. Or that we are here because something wanted us to be.

Of the two possibilities explored in this book, one may begin to feel more coherent with the shape of the world we inhabit. Not by proof, but by resonance. A universe in which freedom exists, in which meaning must be chosen, in which love is possible but never guaranteed—such a world feels less like an accident and more like a gift. If being was given, then silence itself may be a form of trust. And the absence of command may be what allows the presence of compassion, belief, and responsibility to emerge.

The first possibility—emergence without intention—can account for complexity, consciousness, even ethical behavior. But it cannot explain why good and evil should matter beyond function or feeling. It leaves moral experience untethered: real to us, but contingent, evolving, ungrounded. In contrast, if the world was willed into being—not by force, but by a source that gives without commanding—then goodness is not a convention, and evil is not a failure of empathy. They become features of the structure itself. Not imposed, but made possible. In such a world, freedom is not an accident of evolution. It is a condition of the gift.

And if it was given, then the source of that gift cannot be part of the world it gave. It cannot arise from being, or from potential, or from any law it makes possible. It must stand not earlier, not elsewhere—but radically other. Beyond structure, beyond logic, beyond even the possibility of contrast. If intention exists, it must come not from within the system, but from what precedes the very conditions that make a system possible.

It is now ours to live with. Not to resolve, but to live in response to. Through fidelity. Through what we choose to believe, and how we act on what we cannot prove. Through what we protect, what we remember, and what we love. Not as evidence. Not as consolation. But as a way of being in relation to something we cannot possess.

There may never be a final word. But there can be a way of remaining faithful to the question.

That, in the end, is what this book has tried to do. And what remains now is not an answer—but the reader. Still thinking. Still wondering. Still here.

About These References

This book draws upon a wide and deliberately eclectic range of sources, spanning ancient philosophy, contemporary physics, theology, consciousness studies, phenomenology, and metaphysical speculation. The references are not meant to function as authorities in the traditional academic sense, nor do they imply endorsement of any particular system. Rather, they serve as interlocutors—thinkers and texts whose questions, intuitions, and arguments have informed, challenged, or complicated the inquiries explored throughout this work.

Some citations appear multiple times across chapters. This is not an oversight, but a reflection of their ongoing relevance to multiple dimensions of the central question: *Why is there something rather than nothing?* Works by Heidegger, Spinoza, Wittgenstein, Weil, and others recur because they do not offer single answers so much as enduring perspectives—orientations toward being, non-being, freedom, presence, or concealment—that echo differently in various contexts.

Scientific sources are included not only for their empirical insights but also for their metaphysical implications. In particular, cosmology and physics are approached less as explanatory endpoints than as terrains where the boundaries between explanation and mystery become most visible. Similarly, texts on consciousness, intention, and time are not cited as definitive treatments but as provocations—points of departure for reflection.

This bibliography is both a record of influence and an invitation to further reading. Some entries may appear in tension with each other; this is intentional. The project of this book is not to reconcile all positions, but to hold open the space in which multiple frameworks—emergent and intentional, scientific and existential, ancient and modern—can be brought into conversation. The references are therefore part of the method: not footnotes to a fixed thesis, but part of an evolving inquiry that resists final closure.

References – Chapter 1

Albert, D. (2012, March 23). On the origin of everything. *The New York Times Book Review*.

Barrow, J. D. (2000). *The book of nothing: Vacuums, voids, and the latest ideas on the origin of the universe*. Pantheon.

Hawking, S., & Mlodinow, L. (2010). *The grand design*. Bantam.

Heidegger, M. (1996). *Being and time* (J. Stambaugh, Trans.). State University of New York Press. (Original work published 1927)

Heidegger, M. (2000). *Introduction to metaphysics* (G. Fried & R. Polt, Trans.). Yale University Press. (Original work published 1953)

Holt, J. (2012). *Why does the world exist? An existential detective story*. Liveright.

Krauss, L. M. (2012). *A universe from nothing: Why there is something rather than nothing*. Free Press.

Leibniz, G. W. (1989). Principles of nature and grace, based on reason. In R. Ariew & D. Garber (Eds. & Trans.), *Philosophical essays*. Hackett. (Original work published 1714)

Nishitani, K. (1982). *Religion and nothingness* (J. Van Bragt, Trans.). University of California Press.

Nozick, R. (1981). *Philosophical explanations*. Harvard University Press.

Rovelli, C. (2018). *The order of time* (E. Segre & S. Carnell, Trans.). Riverhead Books.

Sokolowski, R. (1995). *The God of faith and reason: Foundations of Christian theology* (2nd ed.). The Catholic University of America Press.

Vilenkin, A. (2006). *Many worlds in one: The search for other universes*. Hill and Wang.

Wilczek, F. (2008). *The lightness of being: Mass, ether, and the unification of forces*. Basic Books.

References – Chapter 2

Al-Farabi. (1985). *On the perfect state* (R. Walzer, Trans.). Oxford University Press. (Original work published ca. 940)

Al-Ghazali. (2000). *The incoherence of the philosophers* (M. E. Marmura, Trans., 2nd ed.). Brigham Young University Press. (Original work published 1095)

Aquinas, T. (2006). *Summa Theologica* (Fathers of the English Dominican Province, Trans.). Christian Classics. (Original work published 1274)

Aristotle. (1984). Physics (R. P. Hardie & R. K. Gaye, Trans.). In J. Barnes (Ed.), *The complete works of Aristotle: The revised Oxford translation* (Vol. 1). Princeton University Press. (Original work ca. 4th century BCE)

Aristotle. (1984). Metaphysics (W. D. Ross, Trans.). In J. Barnes (Ed.), *The *complete works of Aristotle: The revised Oxford translation* (Vol. 2). Princeton University Press. (Original work ca. 4th century BCE)

Augustine. (2008). *Confessions* (H. Chadwick, Trans.). Oxford University Press. (Original work published ca. 400)

Avicenna. (2005). *The metaphysics of The Healing* (M. Marmura, Trans.). Brigham Young University Press. (Original work published ca. 1020)

Bodhi, Bhikkhu, & Ñāṇamoli, Bhikkhu (Trans.). (2000). *The middle length discourses of the Buddha: A translation of the Majjhima Nikāya*. Wisdom Publications.

Camus, A. (1991). *The myth of Sisyphus* (J. O'Brien, Trans.). Vintage International. (Original work published 1942)

Carnap, R. (1959). The elimination of metaphysics through logical analysis of language. In A. J. Ayer (Ed.), *Logical positivism* (pp. 60–81). The Free Press. (Original work published 1932)

Carroll, S. (2016). *The big picture: On the origins of life, meaning, and the universe itself*. Dutton.

de Beauvoir, S. (1948). *The ethics of ambiguity* (B. Frechtman, Trans.). Citadel Press.

Descartes, R. (1984). *Meditations on first philosophy* (D. Cress, Trans.). Hackett Publishing Company. (Original work published 1641)

Guthrie, W. K. C. (1965). *A history of Greek philosophy: Volume 2, The Presocratic tradition from Parmenides to Democritus*. Cambridge University Press.

Hawking, S., & Mlodinow, L. (2010). *The grand design*. Bantam.

Heidegger, M. (1996). *Being and time* (J. Stambaugh, Trans.). State University of New York Press. (Original work published 1927)

Heidegger, M. (1998). What is metaphysics? In D. F. Krell (Ed.), *Basic writings* (Rev. ed., pp. 89–110). HarperCollins. (Original lecture delivered 1929)

Hume, D. (2007). *An enquiry concerning human understanding* (P. Millican, Ed.). Oxford University Press. (Original work published 1748)

Idel, M. (1988). *Kabbalah: New perspectives*. Yale University Press.

Kant, I. (1998). *Critique of pure reason* (P. Guyer & A. W. Wood, Trans.). Cambridge University Press. (Original work published 1781)

Kirk, G. S., Raven, J. E., & Schofield, M. (1983). *The Presocratic philosophers* (2nd ed.). Cambridge University Press.

Krauss, L. M. (2012). *A universe from nothing: Why there is something rather than nothing*. Free Press.

Laozi. (2003). *Dao De Jing: A philosophical translation* (R. T. Ames & D. L. Hall, Trans.). Ballantine Books. (Original work ca. 4th century BCE)

Leibniz, G. W. (1989). *Philosophical essays* (R. Ariew & D. Garber, Eds.). Hackett Publishing Company.

Merleau-Ponty, M. (1962). *Phenomenology of perception* (C. Smith, Trans.). Routledge & Kegan Paul. (Original work published 1945)

Mitchell, D. W. (2002). *Buddhism: Introducing the Buddhist experience*. Oxford University Press.

Nagarjuna. (1995). *The fundamental wisdom of the middle way: Nāgārjuna's Mūlamadhyamakakārikā* (J. L. Garfield, Trans.). Oxford University Press. (Original work ca. 2nd century)

Nicholas of Cusa. (1997). *Of learned ignorance* (H. Lawrence Bond, Trans.). Yale University Press. (Original work published 1440)

Parmenides. (1984). *Parmenides of Elea: A text and translation with an introduction* (D. Gallop, Trans.). University of Toronto Press. (Original work ca. 5th century BCE)

Plato. (1997). Sophist (N. D. White, Trans.). In J. M. Cooper (Ed.), *Plato: Complete works* (pp. 235–293). Hackett.

Plato. (2000). *Timaeus* (D. J. Zeyl, Trans.). Hackett.

Sartre, J.-P. (2001). *Being and nothingness* (H. E. Barnes, Trans.). Routledge. (Original work published 1943)

Scholem, G. (1995). *Major trends in Jewish mysticism* (3rd ed.). Schocken Books.

Scotus, J. D. (1987). *Duns Scotus on the existence of God* (T. Williams, Trans.). Hackett Publishing. (Original work ca. 1300)

Spinoza, B. (1994). *Ethics* (E. Curley, Trans.). Penguin Books. (Original work published 1677)

Tillich, P. (1952). *The courage to be*. Yale University Press.

Watts, A. (1975). *Tao: The watercourse way*. Pantheon Books.

References – Chapter 3

Albert, D. (2012, March 23). On the origin of everything. *The New York Times Book Review*.

Barrow, J. D. (2000). *The book of nothing: Vacuums, voids, and the latest ideas on the origin of the universe*. Pantheon.

Carroll, S. (2016). *The big picture: On the origins of life, meaning, and the universe itself*. Dutton.

Davies, P. (1992). *The mind of God: The scientific basis for a rational world*. Simon & Schuster.

Hawking, S., & Mlodinow, L. (2010). *The grand design*. Bantam.

Heidegger, M. (1996). *Being and time* (J. Stambaugh, Trans.). State University of New York Press. (Original work published 1927)

Heidegger, M. (1998). What is metaphysics? In D. F. Krell (Ed.), *Basic writings* (Rev. ed., pp. 89–110). HarperCollins. (Original lecture delivered 1929)

Holt, J. (2012). *Why does the world exist? An existential detective story*. Liveright.

Krauss, L. M. (2012). *A universe from nothing: Why there is something rather than nothing*. Free Press.

Nozick, R. (1981). *Philosophical explanations*. Harvard University Press.

Parfit, D. (1998). Why anything? Why this? *London Review of Books, 20*(2), 24–27.

Parsons, J. (Ed.). (2019). *The philosophy of nothing*. Routledge.

Rundle, B. (2004). *Why there is something rather than nothing*. Oxford University Press.

Spitzer, R. J. (2010). *New proofs for the existence of God: Contributions of contemporary physics and philosophy*. William B. Eerdmans Publishing Company.

Vilenkin, A. (2006). *Many worlds in one: The search for other universes*. Hill and Wang.

Wilczek, F. (2008). *The lightness of being: Mass, ether, and the unification of forces*. Basic Books.

References – Chapter 4

Anderson, P. W. (1972). More is different. *Science, 177*(4047), 393–396.

Ball, P. (1999). *The self-made tapestry: Pattern formation in nature*. Oxford University Press.

Gödel, K. (1931). Über formal unentscheidbare Sätze der *Principia Mathematica* und verwandter Systeme I. *Monatshefte für Mathematik und Physik, 38*(1), 173–198.

Heisenberg, W. (1958). *Physics and philosophy: The revolution in modern science*. Harper.

Kauffman, S. A. (1995). *At home in the universe: The search for the laws of self-organization and complexity*. Oxford University Press.

Laughlin, R. B. (2005). *A different universe: Reinventing physics from the bottom down*. Basic Books.

Livio, M. (2009). *Is God a mathematician?* Simon & Schuster.

Nagel, E., & Newman, J. R. (2001). *Gödel's proof* (Rev. ed.). New York University Press.

Penrose, R. (2005). *The road to reality: A complete guide to the laws of the universe*. Jonathan Cape.

Plato. (1997). *Complete works* (J. M. Cooper & D. S. Hutchinson, Eds.). Hackett Publishing Company.

Prigogine, I., & Stengers, I. (1984). *Order out of chaos: Man's new dialogue with nature*. Bantam.

Smolin, L. (2013). *Time reborn: From the crisis in physics to the future of the universe*. Houghton Mifflin Harcourt.

Tegmark, M. (2014). *Our mathematical universe: My quest for the ultimate nature of reality*. Alfred A. Knopf.

Wheeler, J. A. (1983). Law without law. In J. A. Wheeler & W. H. Zurek (Eds.), *Quantum theory and measurement*. Princeton University Press.

Wigner, E. P. (1960). The unreasonable effectiveness of mathematics in the natural sciences. *Communications on Pure and Applied Mathematics, 13*(1), 1–14.*

References Chapter 5

Anderson, P. W. (1972). More is different. *Science, 177*(4047), 393–396.

Barrow, J. D. (2007). *New theories of everything: The quest for ultimate explanation*. Oxford University Press.

Becker, A. (2018). *What is real? The unfinished quest for the meaning of quantum physics*. Basic Books.

Bostrom, N. (2003). Are you living in a computer simulation? *The Philosophical Quarterly, 53*(211), 243–255.

Carroll, S. (2016). *The big picture: On the origins of life, meaning, and the universe itself*. Dutton.

Carroll, S. (2019). *Something deeply hidden: Quantum worlds and the emergence of spacetime*. Dutton.

Cartwright, N. (1999). *The dappled world: A study of the boundaries of science*. Cambridge University Press.

Chalmers, D. J. (1996). *The conscious mind: In search of a fundamental theory*. Oxford University Press.

Davies, P. (2007). *The Goldilocks enigma: Why is the universe just right for life?* Houghton Mifflin.

Deacon, T. W. (2011). *Incomplete nature: How mind emerged from matter*. W. W. Norton & Company.

Deutsch, D. (1997). *The fabric of reality: The science of parallel universes—and its implications*. Penguin.

Einstein, A. (1920). *Relativity: The special and general theory*. H. Holt and Company.

Ellis, G. F. R., & Silk, J. (2014). Scientific method: Defend the integrity of physics. *Nature, 516*(7531), 321–323.

Gell-Mann, M. (1994). *The quark and the jaguar: Adventures in the simple and the complex*. W. H. Freeman.

Greene, B. (2004). *The fabric of the cosmos: Space, time, and the texture of reality*. Vintage.

Hawking, S., & Mlodinow, L. (2010). *The grand design*. Bantam Books.

Holland, J. H. (1998). *Emergence: From chaos to order*. Oxford University Press.

Hossenfelder, S. (2018). *Lost in math: How beauty leads physics astray*. Basic Books.

Ladyman, J., & Ross, D. (2007). *Every thing must go: Metaphysics naturalized*. Oxford University Press.

Laughlin, R. B. (2005). *A different universe: Reinventing physics from the bottom down*. Basic Books.

Mitchell, M. (2009). *Complexity: A guided tour*. Oxford University Press.

Penrose, R. (2005). *The road to reality: A complete guide to the laws of the universe*. Vintage.

Rees, M. (1999). *Just six numbers: The deep forces that shape the universe*. Basic Books.

Smolin, L. (2006). *The trouble with physics: The rise of string theory, the fall of a science, and what comes next*. Houghton Mifflin.

Smolin, L. (2013). *Time reborn: From the crisis in physics to the future of the universe*. Houghton Mifflin Harcourt.

Susskind, L. (2005). *The cosmic landscape: String theory and the illusion of intelligent design*. Little, Brown and Company.

Tegmark, M. (2014). *Our mathematical universe: My quest for the ultimate nature of reality*. Vintage.

Weinberg, S. (1992). *Dreams of a final theory: The search for the fundamental laws of nature*. Pantheon.

Wheeler, J. A. (1983). Law without law. In J. A. Wheeler & W. H. Zurek (Eds.), *Quantum theory and measurement* (pp. 182–213). Princeton University Press.

References Chapter 6

Baars, B. J. (1997). *In the theater of consciousness: The workspace of the mind*. Oxford University Press.

Blackmore, S. (2005). *Consciousness: An introduction*. Oxford University Press.

Block, N. (1995). On a confusion about a function of consciousness. *Behavioral and Brain Sciences, 18*(2), 227–247.

Chalmers, D. J. (1995). Facing up to the problem of consciousness. *Journal of Consciousness Studies, 2*(3), 200–219.

Chalmers, D. J. (1996). *The conscious mind: In search of a fundamental theory*. Oxford University Press.

Dehaene, S. (2014). *Consciousness and the brain: Deciphering how the brain codes our thoughts*. Viking.

Dennett, D. C. (1991). *Consciousness explained*. Little, Brown and Company.

Frankish, K. (2016). Illusionism as a theory of consciousness. *Journal of Consciousness Studies, 23*(11–12), 11–39.

Goff, P. (2019). *Galileo's error: Foundations for a new science of consciousness*. Pantheon Books.

Graziano, M. S. A. (2013). *Consciousness and the social brain*. Oxford University Press.

Jackson, F. (1986). What Mary didn't know. *The Journal of Philosophy, 83*(5), 291–295.

James, W. (1890). *The principles of psychology* (Vol. 1). Henry Holt and Company.

Koch, C. (2019). *The feeling of life itself: Why consciousness is widespread but can't be computed*. MIT Press.

Levine, J. (1983). Materialism and qualia: The explanatory gap. *Pacific Philosophical Quarterly, 64*(4), 354–361.

Nagel, T. (1974). What is it like to be a bat? *The Philosophical Review, 83*(4), 435–450.

Russell, B. (2001). *The analysis of mind*. Routledge. (Original work published 1921)

Searle, J. R. (1992). *The rediscovery of the mind*. MIT Press.

Seth, A. K. (2021). *Being you: A new science of consciousness*. Dutton.

Strawson, G. (2006). Realistic monism: Why physicalism entails panpsychism. *Journal of Consciousness Studies, 13*(10–11), 3–31.

Tononi, G. (2008). Consciousness as integrated information: A provisional manifesto. *The Biological Bulletin, 215*(3), 216–242.

Tye, M. (2000). *Consciousness, color, and content*. MIT Press.

Velmans, M. (2009). *Understanding consciousness* (2nd ed.). Routledge.

References Chapter 7

Buber, M. (1970). *I and Thou* (W. Kaufmann, Trans.). Charles Scribner's Sons. (Original work published 1923)

Cobb, J. B., Jr., & Griffin, D. R. (1976). *Process theology: An introductory exposition*. Westminster John Knox Press.

Cooper, J. M. (Ed.). (1997). *Plato: Complete works*. Hackett Publishing.

Hart, D. B. (2013). *The experience of God: Being, consciousness, bliss*. Yale University Press.

Hick, J. (2010). *Evil and the God of love* (Rev. ed.). Palgrave Macmillan.

James, W. (1902). *The varieties of religious experience: A study in human nature*. Longmans, Green, and Co.

Kauffman, S. A. (1995). *At home in the universe: The search for the laws of self-organization and complexity*. Oxford University Press.

Leslie, J., & Kuhn, R. L. (Eds.). (2013). *The mystery of existence: Why is there anything at all?* Wiley-Blackwell.

Lonergan, B. (1957). *Insight: A study of human understanding*. Longmans, Green and Co.

Moser, P. K. (2008). *The elusive God: Reorienting religious epistemology*. Cambridge University Press.

Nagel, T. (2012). *Mind and cosmos: Why the materialist neo-Darwinian conception of nature is almost certainly false*. Oxford University Press.

Peirce, C. S. (1992). *The essential Peirce: Selected philosophical writings* (Vol. 1). Indiana University Press.

Plantinga, A. (1974). *God, freedom, and evil*. Eerdmans.

Plotinus. (1991). *The Enneads* (S. MacKenna, Trans.). Penguin Classics. (Original work ca. 270 CE)

Polkinghorne, J. (1998). *Belief in God in an age of science*. Yale University Press.

Schellenberg, J. L. (2015). *The hiddenness argument: Philosophy's new challenge to belief in God*. Oxford University Press.

Schelling, F. W. J. (1978). *System of transcendental idealism* (P. Heath, Trans.). University of Virginia Press. (Original work published 1800)

Spinoza, B. (1994). *Ethics* (E. Curley, Trans.). Penguin Classics. (Original work published 1677)

Swinburne, R. (2010). *Is there a God?* (Rev. ed.). Oxford University Press.

Tillich, P. (1952). *The courage to be*. Yale University Press.

Weil, S. (2002). *Gravity and grace* (E. Crawford & M. von der Ruhr, Trans.). Routledge.

Wittgenstein, L. (1922). *Tractatus logico-philosophicus* (C. K. Ogden, Trans.). Routledge & Kegan Paul.

References Chapter 8

Bennett, J. (2010). *Vibrant matter: A political ecology of things*. Duke University Press.

Berkeley, G. (2008). *A treatise concerning the principles of human knowledge*. Oxford University Press. (Original work published 1710)

Bohm, D. (1980). *Wholeness and the implicate order*. Routledge.

Chalmers, D. J. (1996). *The conscious mind: In search of a fundamental theory*. Oxford University Press.

Goff, P. (2019). *Galileo's error: Foundations for a new science of consciousness*. Pantheon Books.

Griffin, D. R. (1998). *Unsnarling the world-knot: Consciousness, freedom, and the mind–body problem*. University of California Press.

Harris, A. (2019). *Conscious: A brief guide to the fundamental mystery of the mind*. Harper.

Hoffman, D. D. (2019). *The case against reality: Why evolution hid the truth from our eyes*. W. W. Norton & Company.

James, W. (1904). Does "consciousness" exist? *The Journal of Philosophy, Psychology and Scientific Methods*, *1*(18), 477–491.

Koch, C. (2019). *The feeling of life itself: Why consciousness is widespread but can't be computed*. MIT Press.

Nagel, T. (1974). What is it like to be a bat? *The Philosophical Review*, *83*(4), 435–450.

Nagel, T. (2012). *Mind and cosmos: Why the materialist neo-Darwinian conception of nature is almost certainly false*. Oxford University Press.

Peirce, C. S. (1992). *The essential Peirce: Selected philosophical writings* (Vol. 1). Indiana University Press.

Putnam, H. (1960). Minds and machines. In S. Hook (Ed.), *Dimensions of mind* (pp. 148–180). New York University Press.

Rosenberg, G. (2004). *A place for consciousness: Probing the deep structure of the natural world*. Oxford University Press.

Russell, B. (2001). *The analysis of mind*. Routledge. (Original work published 1921)

Seager, W. (2010). *Theories of consciousness: An introduction and assessment*. Routledge.

Spinoza, B. (1994). *Ethics* (E. Curley, Trans.). Penguin Classics. (Original work published 1677)

Strawson, G. (2006). Realistic monism: Why physicalism entails panpsychism. *Journal of Consciousness Studies*, *13*(10–11), 3–31.

Thompson, E. (2015). *Waking, dreaming, being: Self and consciousness in neuroscience, meditation, and philosophy*. Columbia University Press.

Tononi, G. (2012). *Phi: A voyage from the brain to the soul*. Pantheon.

Varela, F. J., Thompson, E., & Rosch, E. (2016). *The embodied mind: Cognitive science and human experience* (Revised ed.). MIT Press.

Whitehead, A. N. (1978). *Process and reality: An essay in cosmology* (Corrected ed., D. R. Griffin & D. W. Sherburne, Eds.). Free Press.

Wittgenstein, L. (1922). *Tractatus logico-philosophicus* (C. K. Ogden, Trans.). Routledge & Kegan Paul.

References – Chapter 9

Buber, M. (1970). *I and Thou* (W. Kaufmann, Trans.). Charles Scribner's Sons. (Original work published 1923)

Cavell, S. (1979). *The claim of reason: Wittgenstein, skepticism, morality, and tragedy*. Oxford University Press.

Cooper, J. M. (Ed.). (1997). *Plato: Complete works*. Hackett Publishing.

Heschel, A. J. (1951). *Man is not alone: A philosophy of religion*. Farrar, Straus and Giroux.

James, W. (1902). *The varieties of religious experience: A study in human nature*. Longmans, Green, and Co.

Kierkegaard, S. (1991). *Practice in Christianity* (H. V. Hong & E. H. Hong, Trans.). Princeton University Press.

Levinas, E. (1969). *Totality and infinity: An essay on exteriority* (A. Lingis, Trans.). Duquesne University Press.

Lossky, V. (1997). *The mystical theology of the Eastern Church*. St Vladimir's Seminary Press.

Marcel, G. (1950). *The mystery of being* (G. S. Fraser, Trans.). Harvill Press.

Maimonides, M. (1963). *The guide of the perplexed* (S. Pines, Trans.). University of Chicago Press.

Marion, J.-L. (1991). *God without being* (T. A. Carlson, Trans.). University of Chicago Press.

Marion, J.-L. (2002). *Being given: Toward a phenomenology of givenness* (J. L. Kosky, Trans.). Stanford University Press.

Moser, P. K. (2008). *The elusive God: Reorienting religious epistemology*. Cambridge University Press.

Newman, J. H. (1979). *An essay in aid of a grammar of assent*. University of Notre Dame Press. (Original work published 1870)

Pascal, B. (1958). *Pensées* (W. F. Trotter, Trans.). E. P. Dutton. (Original work published 1670)

Polanyi, M. (1962). *Personal knowledge: Towards a post-critical philosophy*. University of Chicago Press.

Pseudo-Dionysius. (1987). *The complete works* (C. Luibheid, Trans.; P. Rorem, Notes & Intro.). Paulist Press.

Ricoeur, P. (1970). *Freud and philosophy: An essay on interpretation* (D. Savage, Trans.). Yale University Press.

Schellenberg, J. L. (2015). *The hiddenness argument: Philosophy's new challenge to belief in God*. Oxford University Press.

Sells, M. A. (1994). *Mystical languages of unsaying*. University of Chicago Press.

Taylor, C. (2007). *A secular age*. Belknap Press of Harvard University Press.

Turner, D. (1995). *The darkness of God: Negativity in Christian mysticism*. Cambridge University Press.

Weil, S. (1951). *Waiting for God* (E. Craufurd, Trans.). Harper & Brothers.

Weil, S. (2002). *Gravity and grace* (E. Crawford & M. von der Ruhr, Trans.). Routledge.

Williams, R. (2014). *The edge of words: God and the habits of language.* Bloomsbury.

Wittgenstein, L. (1922). *Tractatus logico-philosophicus* (C. K. Ogden, Trans.). Routledge & Kegan Paul.

References – Chapter 10

Buber, M. (1970). *I and Thou* (W. Kaufmann, Trans.). Charles Scribner's Sons. (Original work published 1923)

Camus, A. (1991). *The myth of Sisyphus* (J. O'Brien, Trans.). Vintage International. (Original work published 1942)

Frankfurt, H. G. (2004). *The reasons of love.* Princeton University Press.

Frankl, V. E. (2006). *Man's search for meaning* (I. Lasch, Trans.). Beacon Press. (Original work published 1946)

Heschel, A. J. (1951). *Man is not alone: A philosophy of religion.* Farrar, Straus and Giroux.

Kierkegaard, S. (1980). *The concept of anxiety: A simple psychologically orienting deliberation on the dogmatic issue of hereditary sin* (R. Thomte & A. B. Anderson, Trans.). Princeton University Press. (Original work published 1844)

Kierkegaard, S. (1995). *Works of love* (H. V. Hong & E. H. Hong, Trans.). Princeton University Press. (Original work published 1847)

Levinas, E. (1969). *Totality and infinity: An essay on exteriority* (A. Lingis, Trans.). Duquesne University Press.

MacIntyre, A. (2007). *After virtue: A study in moral theory* (3rd ed.). University of Notre Dame Press. (Original work published 1981)

Marion, J.-L. (2002). *Being given: Toward a phenomenology of givenness* (J. L. Kosky, Trans.). Stanford University Press.

Murdoch, I. (1970). *The sovereignty of good.* Routledge.

Nussbaum, M. C. (2001). *The fragility of goodness: Luck and ethics in Greek tragedy and philosophy* (Rev. ed.). Cambridge University Press. (Original work published 1986)

Ricoeur, P. (1995). *Figuring the sacred: Religion, narrative, and imagination* (D. Pellauer, Trans.). Fortress Press.

Taylor, C. (1989). *Sources of the self: The making of the modern identity.* Harvard University Press.

Tillich, P. (2000). *The courage to be.* Yale University Press. (Original work published 1952)

Weil, S. (2002). *Gravity and grace* (E. Crawford & M. von der Ruhr, Trans.). Routledge.

Williams, B. (1985). *Ethics and the limits of philosophy.* Harvard University Press.

Wittgenstein, L. (1953). *Philosophical investigations* (G. E. M. Anscombe, Trans.). Blackwell.

Wolf, S. (2010). *Meaning in life and why it matters*. Princeton University Press.

References Chapter 11

Arendt, H. (1958). *The human condition*. University of Chicago Press.

Bachelard, G. (1964). *The poetics of space* (M. Jolas, Trans.). Beacon Press. (Original work published 1958)

Camus, A. (1991). *The myth of Sisyphus* (J. O'Brien, Trans.). Vintage International. (Original work published 1942)

Frankl, V. E. (2006). *Man's search for meaning* (I. Lasch, Trans.). Beacon Press. (Original work published 1946)

Heidegger, M. (1962). *Being and time* (J. Macquarrie & E. Robinson, Trans.). Harper & Row. (Original work published 1927)

Merleau-Ponty, M. (1962). *Phenomenology of perception* (C. Smith, Trans.). Routledge & Kegan Paul. (Original work published 1945)

Ricoeur, P. (2004). *Memory, history, forgetting* (K. Blamey & D. Pellauer, Trans.). University of Chicago Press.

Tillich, P. (1952). *The courage to be*. Yale University Press.

Weil, S. (2002). *Gravity and grace* (E. Crawford & M. von der Ruhr, Trans.). Routledge.

Yalom, I. D. (2008). *Staring at the sun: Overcoming the terror of death*. Jossey-Bass.

References Chapter 12

Becker, E. (1973). *The denial of death*. Free Press.

Frankl, V. E. (2006). *Man's search for meaning* (I. Lasch, Trans.). Beacon Press. (Original work published 1946)

Heidegger, M. (1962). *Being and time* (J. Macquarrie & E. Robinson, Trans.). Harper & Row. (Original work published 1927)

Jonas, H. (1992). *Mortality and morality: A search for the good after Auschwitz* (L. Vogel, Ed.). Northwestern University Press.

Kübler-Ross, E. (1969). *On death and dying*. Macmillan.

Levinas, E. (1985). *Ethics and infinity: Conversations with Philippe Nemo* (R. A. Cohen, Trans.). Duquesne University Press.

Ricoeur, P. (2004). *Memory, history, forgetting* (K. Blamey & D. Pellauer, Trans.). University of Chicago Press.

Solomon, S., Greenberg, J., & Pyszczynski, T. (2015). *The worm at the core: On the role of death in life*. Random House.

Tillich, P. (1952). *The courage to be*. Yale University Press.

Yalom, I. D. (2008). *Staring at the sun: Overcoming the terror of death*. Jossey-Bass.

References Chapter 13

Buber, M. (1970). *I and Thou* (W. Kaufmann, Trans.). Charles Scribner's Sons. (Original work published 1923)

Frankl, V. E. (2006). *Man's search for meaning* (I. Lasch, Trans.). Beacon Press. (Original work published 1946)

Halbwachs, M. (1992). *On collective memory* (L. A. Coser, Ed. & Trans.). University of Chicago Press.

Kearney, R. (2002). *On stories*. Routledge.

Levinas, E. (1969). *Totality and infinity: An essay on exteriority* (A. Lingis, Trans.). Duquesne University Press.

Marcel, G. (1964). *The mystery of being: Volume 2, Faith and reality* (R. Rosthal, Trans.). St. Augustine's Press.

Ricoeur, P. (1986). *Fallible man* (C. A. Kelbley, Trans.). Fordham University Press.

Taylor, C. (1989). *Sources of the self: The making of the modern identity*. Harvard University Press.

Weil, S. (2002). *Gravity and grace* (E. Crawford & M. von der Ruhr, Trans.). Routledge.

Wyschogrod, E. (1998). *An ethics of remembrance: History, heterology, and the nameless others*. Stanford University Press.

References – Chapter 14

Bachelard, G. (1964). *The poetics of space* (M. Jolas, Trans.). Beacon Press. (Original work published 1958)

Buber, M. (1970). *I and Thou* (W. Kaufmann, Trans.). Charles Scribner's Sons. (Original work published 1923)

Camus, A. (1991). *The myth of Sisyphus* (J. O'Brien, Trans.). Vintage International. (Original work published 1942)

Frankl, V. E. (2006). *Man's search for meaning* (I. Lasch, Trans.). Beacon Press. (Original work published 1946)

Heidegger, M. (1962). *Being and time* (J. Macquarrie & E. Robinson, Trans.). Harper & Row. (Original work published 1927)

Levinas, E. (1985). *Ethics and infinity: Conversations with Philippe Nemo* (R. A. Cohen, Trans.). Duquesne University Press.

Marcel, G. (1964). *The mystery of being: Volume 2, Faith and reality* (R. Rosthal, Trans.). St. Augustine's Press.

Merleau-Ponty, M. (1962). *Phenomenology of perception* (C. Smith, Trans.). Routledge & Kegan Paul. (Original work published 1945)

Ricoeur, P. (2004). *Memory, history, forgetting* (K. Blamey & D. Pellauer, Trans.). University of Chicago Press.

Rilke, R. M. (2004). *Letters to a young poet* (M. D. Herter Norton, Trans.). W. W. Norton & Company.

Weil, S. (1951). *Waiting for God* (E. Craufurd, Trans.). Harper & Brothers.

Weil, S. (2002). *Gravity and grace* (E. Crawford & M. von der Ruhr, Trans.). Routledge.

Wittgenstein, L. (1953). *Philosophical investigations* (G. E. M. Anscombe, Trans.). Blackwell.

www.ingramcontent.com/pod-product-compliance
Lightning Source LLC
Chambersburg PA
CBHW031530120626
46545CB00005B/2076